THE PORTUGAL OF SALAZAR

THE
PORTUGAL OF SALAZAR

By

MICHAEL DERRICK

LONDON
SANDS: THE PALADIN PRESS
15 KING STREET, COVENT GARDEN, W.C.2
AND AT GLASGOW

PRINTED IN GUERNSEY, C.I., BRITISH ISLES,
BY THE STAR AND GAZETTE LTD. FOR
SANDS: THE PALADIN PRESS, 15 KING ST.,
COVENT GARDEN, LONDON, W.C. 2

FIRST PUBLISHED 1938

CONTENTS

" WE DO NOT ASK FOR MUCH.   AN UNDERSTAND-
ING AND CONSCIOUSNESS OF THE FATHERLAND
AND OF NATIONAL UNITY; OF THE FAMILY, THE
PRIMARY SOCIAL UNIT; OF AUTHORITY AND OF
OBEDIENCE TO AUTHORITY; OF THE SPIRITUAL
VALUES OF LIFE AND OF THE RESPECT THAT IS
OWING TO MAN; OF THE OBLIGATION TO LABOUR;
OF VIRTUE AND OF THE SACRED NATURE OF RELI-
GION—THAT IS WHAT IS ESSENTIAL IN THE MEN-
TAL AND MORAL FORMATION OF A CITIZEN OF
THE ' ESTADO NOVO '.

" WE ARE OPPOSED TO ALL THE INTERNATIONAL-
ISMS, OPPOSED TO COMMUNISM, TO SOCIALISM, TO
LIBERTARIAN SYNDICALISM; WE ARE OPPOSED TO
ALL THAT DISINTEGRATES, DIVIDES, OR DISSOLVES
THE FAMILY; WE ARE OPPOSED TO THE CLASS
STRUGGLE. WE ARE AGAINST THOSE WHO KNOW
NO COUNTRY AND NO GOD; AGAINST THE BONDAGE
OF THE WORKERS, AGAINST THE PURELY MATE-
RIALIST CONCEPTION OF LIFE, AGAINST THE IDEA
THAT MIGHT IS RIGHT. WE ARE AGAINST ALL
THE GREAT HERESIES OF OUR AGE, ALL THE MORE
BECAUSE WE HAVE YET TO BE CONVINCED THAT
THERE IS ANY PART OF THE WORLD WHERE
LIBERTY TO PROPAGATE SUCH HERESIES HAS BEEN
THE CAUSE OF ANYTHING GOOD: SUCH LIBERTY, IN
THE HANDS OF THE BARBARIANS OF MODERN TIMES,
SERVES ONLY TO UNDERMINE THE FOUNDATIONS
OF OUR CIVILISATION."

OLIVEIRA SALAZAR

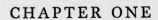

CHAPTER ONE

CHAPTER ONE

INTRODUCTORY

OUR generation has witnessed the final collapse of the economic Liberalism which prevailed in the nineteenth century; and with our generation and the next lies the task of reconstructing Europe. Internationally, the period of unrestricted private enterprise and competition has ended in deadlock and confusion. And in all countries capitalism has left as its legacy a class of property-less and irresponsible workers, destined, despite an overproduction resulting from unique technical achievement, to lead sub-human existences in conditions of poverty and squalor.

The age of *laissez-faire, laissez-passer,* has of necessity given place to an age of planned economy; and parallel to the collapse of economic Liberalism has been the failure of political Liberalism. In their place the new totalitarian ideologies are emerging. There is the Marxist totalitarianism, which would eliminate from society all classes save the workers and from life all spiritual values, and would itself provide the be-all and the end-all of human existence; and there is the totalitarianism of the new nationalisms, which would discipline the individual to an almost mystical conception of the State.

The conflict of ideologies to-day presents the gravest threat to the peace of the world; but there is one man in Europe who, more than any other, has shown that totalitarianism is not the only alternative to undisciplined individualism, class exploitation, and the rule of plutocracy, and that there is a possible form of social and economic Order that is not the impersonal order of the new ideologies. Oliveira Salazar has, during the past ten years, brought into being in Portugal a Christian and Corporate State which provides justice for the long-exploited working classes without preaching the appalling doctrine of the class war, which provides order in the nation without arrogating to the State functions which do not properly belong to it, and which appeals to Nationalism with due regard for the responsibilities of the Nation as a component part of a common European whole.

The Corporate conception of society is in its essence as old as Europe and the Faith, and the neo-Corporatism of Salazar is no more than an attempt to supersede what is known as Capitalism by building according to the principles that were rejected when Capitalism began. In its essence it is no more than an organic conception of society which does not forget the Rights of Man, but which remembers also what have for so long been forgotten: the Duties of Man. The component parts of society are disciplined, but they are self-disciplined; the State regulates the common whole in the common good, but "the State is no more than an artificial mechanism at the service of that natural organism which is the community: those who in it exercise power have only duties towards society, which alone has rights ".[1] The medieval Guilds were corporate bodies, integral parts of society, alike protecting their members from others and others from their members. Neo-corporatism seeks to restore such bodies to society, in some form suitable to the very changed needs and conditions of contemporary life and civilisation. It seeks to reassert that every Right can be expressed conversely as a Duty, and that every man has a duty towards his neighbour, towards the community into which he was born.

The Corporate State of the New Portugal, of the Portugal of Salazar, is an attempt towards the establishment of that " sane corporative system " of which Pope Pius XI speaks,[2] the principles of which have long been advocated by the Catholic school of de Mun and Vogelsang and de la Tour du Pin. But it is an ideal towards which even in England we have witnessed many approaches from various angles. We have seen the Guild Socialists, led by Mr. A. J. Penty and Mr. A. R. Orage, whose ideas may be traced back to Ruskin. Maitland introduced into England the writings of Otto Gierke, who taught the organic nature, the Real Personality, of the integral parts of society. And Professor Maynard Keynes has expressed himself in favour of a form of economic organisation remarkably close to the system of corporations: rather than State Socialism he would see " the growth of semi-autonomous bodies within the State—bodies whose criterion of action within their own field is solely the public good as they understand it, and from whose deliberations motives of private advantage are excluded—bodies which in the ordinary course of affairs are mainly autonomous within their prescribed limitations, but are subject in the last resort to the sovereignty of the democracy expressed through Parliament ".[3]

Thanks chiefly to misuse of the word " Fascism " by left-wing propaganda, there is a general impression abroad that Corporatism implies Imperialism, or a conviction that guns are more necessary than butter. It is not accurate to refer to Germany as a Corporate State; Italy is a Corporate State, but she appears to reject the international aspect of the corporate principle. Internationally, she still seems to plead *laissez-faire, laissez-passer*. Nor is it true that Corporatism implies *étatisme*, or economic nationalism, or any form of neo-paganism. What it does imply it is the purpose of this book to tell, for in contemporary Portugal may be seen the truest attempt that has yet been made towards a realisation of corporative theory. There is Fascist corporatism in Italy and pseudo-corporatism in Germany; there is crippled corporatism in Austria, there are the beginnings of corporatism in Switzerland, and there has been corporative experiment in Bulgaria and elsewhere. But the work of Salazar constitutes an experiment unique in modern Europe.

It is true that since the summer of 1936 the war in Spain has given rise in Portugal to a state of national emergency, which has compelled Salazar to take some measures that he would not have countenanced during the eight years of comparative tranquillity in which he held office previous to that war. Conditions of national danger do not permit any political experiment to take its natural course, least of all one which seeks to reduce the functions of the State to a minimum. It is the threat from the German frontier that has crippled the corporative experiment of Schuschnigg and the martyred Dollfuss in Austria. But Salazar did enough during those eight years to show that he is bringing into being in Portugal a genuine corporatism; a *corporatisme d'association*, as distinct from a *corporatisme d'état*. It is not true to say of the New Portugal that the State has arrogated to itself anything beyond the things which are Caesar's.

Europe to-day is threatened with a war of ideologies. But the real and ultimate issue is not the issue between Fascism and Communism. That is not the issue in Spain. Fascism is something Italian, as Naziism is something German and Soviet Communism something Oriental; whatever emerges in Spain will be different from all of these, as essentially Spanish as the Portugal of Salazar is Portuguese. The issue that is being fought to the death in Spain is the issue which is before Europe. It is this: will that which emerges be Christian, or will it be pagan or (which is worse) purely atheist and anthropocentric? It can be put as simply as that. Those who condone the Spanish Government against which General Franco has led Spain in revolt think it is merely godless; those who fear it think it hates God. At present there is every indication that Franco will win.

That is the second important reason why consideration should be given to the Portugal of Salazar. When Franco has won, there will be an inevitable period of martial law; for a long time there must be sporadic unrest, and guerilla warfare will be carried on in the eastern provinces. But gradually the New Spain will emerge; and there is every indication that it will follow closely the lines of the New Portugal.[4] Franco is a man much nearer in blood, and probably much nearer in every way, to Salazar than to Mussolini. He will be influenced much more by the Spanish and Portuguese integral corporativists, and even by men like Bottai and Manoïlesco the Rumanian, than by the model of Italian Fascism. At all events, no clearer idea of what the Spanish Nationalists are fighting to achieve in the material order can be gained than by studying the Portugal of Salazar. Every political experiment must be conditioned by the nature of the people with whom it is concerned. There are many different peoples in the Iberian Peninsula, of whom the Portuguese are one. They are much more akin to the Castilians than are the Catalans, but Castile is the heart of Spain. Any Corporate State that arises in Spain will take its nature from the people of Spain, and will be closely akin to the Corporate State of the neighbouring people of Portugal.

There is no natural frontier between Spain and Portugal, and, although, with the exception of a brief period at the close of the sixteenth century, Portugal has been an independent nation for eight centuries, there are, apart from history, no greater reasons for her independence than there are for the independence of Catalonia or the Spanish Basques. That is not to say that it would not be a terrible crime if Portugal were forcibly incorporated in Spain. But General Franco is the declared opponent of regional autonomies in Spain, and reports have reached Lisbon of maps seen pinned to the wall at military headquarters at Burgos and Salamanca in which Portugal appears as a Province of Spain. It is unlikely that there is substance in these reports, or that General Franco intends at any date to challenge Portuguese independence. Nevertheless, the possibility cannot be ruled out. If when the civil was is over, General Franco proves to be unduly under the influence of Italy, as is feared by many; and if Italy is then still continuing her policy of opposing British naval power in the Mediterranean, it is conceivable that, after an interval for national recuperation, a military offensive against Portugal will be launched. For the basis of Portuguese Foreign Policy is and will remain her British alliance. The mouth of the Tagus provides what is probably the finest natural harbour in Europe, and it has been virtually at the disposal of the British fleet ever since Britain had an interest in the Mediterranean. The harbours of Portugal are of the utmost importance to any Power concerned in the Mediterranean; indeed, according to Mr. H. A. L. Fisher, "Lisbon is the key to the Mediterranean."[5]

In the possible but, it is hoped, improbable event of an Italo-Spanish offensive being launched against Portugal at some future date, Great Britain will therefore be vitally interested. Moreover, she will be bound by treaty to go to the assistance of Portugal.

In speculating thus about the possible evil results to Portugal of excessive Italian influence accompanying a Nationalist victory in Spain, it should not be forgotten that the victory of international Communism would have presented her with a much more certain menace. "A union of Iberian Soviet republics—that is our aim," said Largo Caballero to the American journalist Edward Knoblaugh. "The Iberian peninsula will again be one country. Portugal will come in, peaceably we hope, but by force if necessary. . . . Lenin declared Spain would be the second Soviet Republic in Europe. Lenin's prophecy will come true. I shall be the second Lenin who shall make it come true." If any such onslaught had been made, Portugal would equally have had the right to demand the intervention of Great Britain. Let this be remembered by those who so bitterly denounce General Franco, the defender of Portugal as well as of Spain from the Comintern.

There is no doubt that the present years are extremely critical ones for Portugal, and the Anglo-Portuguese alliance provides the third important reason why attention should be given in England to Salazar and his work. That alliance is the oldest in Europe. On October 25, 1937, Lisbon celebrated the seven hundred and ninetieth anniversary of the first co-operation of the English with the Portuguese against a common foe.

In 1147 Affonso Henriquez, the first King of Portugal, took Lisbon from the Moors, with the assistance of some English Knights on their way to the second Crusade, and an English monk of Winchelsea became the first Bishop of Lisbon. The citadel then captured is still known as the Castle of St. George. Six centuries ago, on May 9, 1386, the English and Portuguese signed a Treaty at Windsor, "for ever"; and although the alliance dates really only from the time of Cromwell, it has endured to this day: the destinies of two Atlantic European nations have been linked together. The English navigators followed the great Portuguese discoverers of the age of Prince Henry the Navigator (whose mother was an English woman) to found the British Empire. When a Portuguese princess of the Royal House of Braganza married Charles II of England, she brought to England as her dowry Bombay, an important base in India, and Tangier, which was England's first naval base in the Mediterranean. The alliance was renewed a generation later by the Methuen Treaty, and the English gentry, to the great detriment of their health but to the benefit of an historic friendship, began to drink port instead of claret. A century later, British and Portuguese fought together to drive Napoleon from the Peninsula, and in 1916 they were fighting together in Flanders. To-day the alliance is as secure as ever, and is strengthened by important commercial bonds. In February 1938, a British naval and military mission will visit Portugal to investigate the present possibilities of collaboration in war should the necessity arise.

The connections between Great Britain and Portugal, then, are of the closest. In 1933, when the new Portuguese Constitution was approved by a national plebiscite, *The Times* wrote in a leading article that "the course of the new régime will be followed with the greatest sympathy and interest in this country ".[6] That was nearly five years ago; yet practically no public interest has been shown; while public sympathy has been steadily diminishing ever since war broke out in Spain and the Comintern began to put about the legend, at once accepted, that Portugal is

" Fascist " and a satellite state of Italy. Despite the prophecy of *The Times*, this brief book represents the first attempt that has been made by an Englishman to understand and to describe the mind and work of Salazar.

It is its purpose to indicate what is the real nature of contemporary Portugal. It will attempt also to indicate what contemporary Portugal is not. M. Mihaïl Manoïlesco has done some valuable debunking in his book *Le Siècle du Corporatisme*.[7] He makes clear five important things about corporatism:

(1) That modern corporatism must necessarily be very different from, and is not to be confused with, the medieval Guild system.

(2) That it cannot be confounded with Fascism, in spite of the progress which, in the exclusively economic form, it has made under that régime.

(3) That it is not a hypocritical instrument for the consolidation of the existing social conditions with all their iniquities.

(4) That it does not restrict itself to the organisation of the material forces of the nation only, but that it constitutes the sole means of integrating every aspect of the national life.

(5) That it does not mean the mobilisation of the egotism of groups against the national interest, but, on the contrary, the acceptance of the principle of the common good.

We would not say that we agree in all things with M. Manoïlesco; and we think, for instance, that Salazar would not countenance the degree of *étatisme* that appears in his exposition of corporative theory. Nevertheless, these five caveats must be borne well in mind by all who would understand the corporatism of Portugal and Salazar.

II

PORTUGAL

Portugal has an area on the mainland of Europe of 34,254 square miles, and an Atlantic coastline of some 350 miles. Her population in 1930 was 6,826,000, and is to-day probably about seven millions, since the birth-rate, although declining, is still substantially higher than the death-rate.[8] Although in area she is about the same, her population is therefore considerably greater than that of Ireland. In many ways, however, Portugal may be compared to Ireland: she looks out on to the Atlantic from the western edge of Europe, and her people are people of the Celtic fringe. Many travellers have been reminded of the Irish by the Portuguese, and to many the Portuguese landscape has been strangely reminiscent of Ireland. Thus Mr. Douglas Goldring wrote recently: " Portugal is a small, compact, and manageable (*sic*) country about the size of Ireland, which in a queer indefinite way it resembles. At least, I found myself constantly thinking of Ireland as I travelled through it, although the differences between the two countries are ob-

23

vious."[9]   Or again, Mr. Aubrey Bell writes in what
has become a standard work about the Portuguese[10]:
"In some measure, those who know the Irish peasant
know the Portuguese. . . . Indeed, if you take the
Irish peasantry, add hot sun, a spice of the East, and
perhaps something of the negro's vanity and slight
hold on life, you have the Portuguese.   The quick
intelligence, the dreaming melancholy, the slyness
and love of intrigue, the wit and imagination are here,
and the power of expression in words.   Generosity,
too, and habits as unpractical as could be desired."

And since this is a book about the present condition
of Portugal, rather than about the Portuguese people,
we will leave it at that: that none can know the Portuguese without visiting their country, but that those
who know the Irish will know also the Portuguese in
some degree.

You get very different types in different parts of
the country, of course—the dwellers in the high lands
of Beira and the Minho and Tras os Montes; the
farmers of the Alemtejo, the land beyond the Tagus;
the excitable *algarvios* of the south; and so on—but
the Portuguese have been an independent people for
eight centuries, with the exception of sixty uneasy
years between 1580 and 1640, and that could not have
been so had they not been a race apart from Spain.
There are many peoples in Spain, and it is impossible
to say (I write in December 1937) when again they will
live under a common rule; but the Portuguese are
different from them all.

We will not attempt to trace their racial pedigree:
that would be impossible.   The Portuguese have been
all over the world, and all over the world they have

intermarried with their native dependents. The Celt-Iberian stock of Portugal survived the centuries of Moorish overlords as it had survived the overlordship of Romans and Visigoths: but into that Celt-Iberian stock has been infused a surprising amount of negroid blood. The *Chronicles of Azurara*[11] describe how the systematic introduction of African negroes into Portugal dates from the time of Henry the Navigator. Right up to the end of the eighteenth century all the big families of Portugal had large numbers of negro servants, and, in the almost complete absence of that colour prejudice so characteristic of the Anglo-Saxons, a definite negroid strain in the Portuguese people has resulted. To-day there is in Africa a great contrast between the way the Portuguese and British regard their black colonials. A result is that the Portuguese for centuries retained their colonial Empire without the help of any considerable army. It is rare to-day to meet a coloured man in Portugal, or even in Lisbon; but the negroid strain is very often apparent. It would not be an altogether bad thing if Portuguese nationalism to-day became infected with a little of the racial madness that characterises the nationalism of Germany, for their extremely mixed blood is an undoubted source of weakness to the race. However, it accentuates the contrast with the Spanish.

Spain is a Mediterranean country, but Portugal looks out upon the Atlantic. The Spanish conquistadores and the English discoverers of the sixteenth century followed where the Portuguese led; it is the Atlantic that has made the greatness of Portugal. To-day, although the Portuguese have yet to produce great airmen, Lisbon provides the starting-place for the most important north Atlantic crossing by air, and the Portuguese Azores a half-way house.

Spain turns her life towards her great Mediterranean coast that runs from Cape Cervera to the Straits of Gibraltar; her Atlantic coastline is no more than a narrow strip, separated from the interior by the Cantabrian mountains. She is so big and her life is so various that she is almost complete as a continent by herself; and she is isolated from Europe by the Pyrenees. Portugal looks out upon the Ocean, and is linked by the Ocean to Europe: she is the little Europe beyond Spain. Her culture is Romano-Celtic rather than Iberian.

The reconquest of Portugal from the Moors took place eight centuries ago: the first King of Portugal was the half-legendary Affonso Henriquez, who proclaimed himself after the famous battle of Ourique in 1139. The nation reached the frontiers which are hers to-day during the reign of Affonso III (1248-1279); and a long period of intermittent warfare with Leon and Castile ended with the battle of Ajubarrota, in 1385, from which dates the complete independence of Portugal. That battle was won by João I, first King of the House of Aviz, and father by his English wife of Prince Henry the Navigator.

During the whole of the fourteenth century a vigorous civilisation was developing in Portugal; and in particular that splendid tradition of seamanship which was to be the national glory was being steadily built up. Under João I the period of maritime expansion began, with the conquest of Ceuta in 1415; but it was under the inspiration of his son, Prince Henry the Navigator, that Portugal discovered the world for Europe. The story of Bartolomeo Diaz and Vasco de Gama, of Affonso Albuquerque and Duarte Pacheco Pereira, has been told often enough by historians since it was sung in epic verse by Camoës, the national poet: it cannot be told again here. The Portuguese were the first Europeans to round the Cape, the first to reach India; as the colonisers of Brazil, they shared with the Spanish the discovery of the new world. The Portugal of Salazar has the memory of her great age in her colonial Empire.

The Portuguese Empire of to-day represents a total area of over 850,000 square miles, which is about twenty-five times the size of Portugal in Europe. That is a fact now looked upon by the Germans with a jealous eye; although it must be remembered that there are three other European powers whose foreign possessions are proportionately more extensive.

In Europe, Portugal has the archipelagoes of Madeira and the Azores, which are regarded for administrative purposes as provinces of the mainland. In Africa she has the extremely valuable territories of Angola on the west coast and Mozambique on the east. She has also Cabinda, a small piece of the coastline of the Belgian Congo, and Guinea; and off the west coast she owns a considerable number of islands, of which the most important are the Cape Verde Islands, the Bissagos Islands, Prince's Island, and St. Thomas. On the west coast of India she still has Goa, to which she proudly refers as "The State of India", and which is the only part of India not under British sovereignty. In the East Indies she shares the island of Timor with the Dutch, and in China she has

Macao, a trading station opposite Hong-Kong at the mouth of the Si-Kiang River.

The problems and affairs of the Portuguese Empire are outside the scope of this book. Its present position and the principles to be observed in its administration are defined in the Colonial Act of July 8, 1930, which was drawn up by Dr. Salazar, who temporarily assumed the Ministry of Colonies for that purpose; and, by Article CXXXIII of the Constitution of 1933, " the provisions of the Colonial Act shall be regarded as constitutional matter ". The very pressing colonial problem was then vigorously tackled by a brilliant Colonial Minister, Dr. Armindo Monteiro. Dr. Monteiro is now ambassador in London, and when an honorary degree was recently conferred upon him by the University of Oxford, the Public Orator described him as " a second founder of the Portuguese Colonial Empire ".

The Colonial Act, with its later complementary laws, is an application of the corporative theory of Dr. Salazar which it is the chief purpose of this book to discuss. As the nation is an organic whole, so is the Empire. The colonies are bound to co-operate, as are the corporative bodies, as members of the same commonwealth; but the greatest possible measure of autonomy is to be given to each colonial government, as to each corporation. The underlying idea is decentralisation so far as is consonant with a high sense of common destiny and a common responsibility. The corporative organisation of each colony has not yet been carried very far, but its main bases were defined early in 1937 by Decree-Law No. 27552. From the preamble to that we may quote a significant passage, since in the matter of the colonial Empire we have found a brief preliminary reflection of the corporatism of Salazar. "The time has come to lay down the principles of Colonial Corporativism. The principles formulated are purposely broad and general, so as to be applicable to existing conditions. The Government have no wish to formulate cast-iron regulations which subsequently might be found to be impracticable or prejudicial, and desires principally to co-ordinate the economic activity of the colonies so that the highest possible results may be secured. There is no claim of infallibility made for schemes outlined in the present Decree-Law. They may have to be altered, added to, or even replaced by others, as actual practice shall dictate."

In that paragraph we see illustrated one of the greatest strengths of the *Estado Novo* : that is, its avoidance of a "cast-iron" system, and its continual and frank acknowledgment that its present stage is purely experimental. That is one of the chief reasons why the *Estado Novo*, the Portugal of Salazar, will live.

The Portugal of Salazar is a Christian and Corporate State. The purpose of this book is to give some indication of what that means, both objectively, in describing the principles on which it is built, how they are Christian and, in the truest sense of that much-abused word, democratic, and how it differs from the experiments in national reconstruction that are in process in Italy and Germany; and subjectively, in describing how it represents a vindication of the historic Portugal, a truly national resurrection after a century in which an alien and artificial Liberalism reduced the country to chaos. The *Estado Novo* is essentially Christian: it is also essentially Portuguese.

The Englishman who can think of a national revival only in terms of what is known as "the standard of living", or of trade balance, or of public works, will be surprised to find little reference to such criteria in this book. To many, Dr. Salazar is known only as one of the most brilliant Finance Ministers of modern times. It was in that capacity that he first entered public life. He found his country mortgaged and bankrupt: he has set her affairs in order for the first time for centuries, and has made her "almost independent of international finance ".[1] In any country his financial administration would have been remarkable; in Portugal, it is almost miraculous.

On a basis of sound finance an extensive programme of public works has been undertaken. Motor roads have been made throughout a country which previously was almost inaccessible except by mule. In telegraphic and telephonic communications, in education, in railways, in harbour works, and in housing, much has been done. But we shall not assess Portugal's debt to Dr. Salazar in terms of reinforced concrete.

CHAPTER TWO

CHAPTER TWO

I

THE RECORD OF THE REPUBLIC

IT is the purpose of this book to describe what Portugal is like to-day, rather than what she has been like in the past. But it is not possible to discuss Salazar without placing him in his historical context, and particularly in his context in recent Portuguese history. The only way to introduce Salazar is to give some idea of the Portugal into which he was born and in which he grew up; we will go back to the last years of the Monarchy, when he was a boy being educated at a seminary in Upper Beira.

On May 18, 1906, Carlos I, King of Portugal, did that which led directly to his murder two years later: he gave charge of the Portuguese Government to a man who represented neither of the two parties which had for long been alternating in power. For years the *Regeneradores* and the *Progressistas*, each a political gang depending on demagogy, corruption, and *caciquismo*, or the support of petty tyrants, had played the political game unchallenged. The country, says the *Cambridge Modern History*, was "governed by contending factions of professional politicians, who have no other care than their own immediate personal advantage ".[1] That is understatement. The politicians at San Bento had this care, that their machinations should not interfere with the oligarchy that exploited the nation. The perpetual political puppet-show was no more than a drop-scene, a sordid scramble that concealed the unchallenged sway of the rich, while the people starved and the nation drifted more and more into the control of foreign bond-holders. The system was ostensibly Liberal democracy on the English pattern; in fact it was the worst kind of government by oligarchy.

This state of affairs was challenged in May 1906, by King Carlos, when he called to power a man named Franco, which word means "Free". He had the temerity publicly to express the hope that this man might prove strong enough to administer the nation in the national interest. The immediate result was a great storm of protest, and the redoubling of efforts to secure the overthrow of the Monarchy. Chief among the Republicans were the Freemasons of the Portuguese Grand Orient, who had long sought to install a completely Masonic oligarchy, and whose organisation was both formidable and extensive. In the elections of August, four important Republican deputies were returned to the Cortès, including António José de Almeida, who had led the Masonic revolution in Oporto in 1891, and Affonso Costa, leader of the Carbonarios, the terrorist forces of Masonry, and of the "White Ants", his own particular organisation, editor of the Republican newspaper *O Mundo*, and probably the most unscrupulous demagogue that Portugal has ever known. By May

34

1907, there was complete political deadlock, and the King was faced with the alternatives of dismissing Franco or dissolving the Cortès. On May 10th he dissolved the Cortès, and João Franco stood alone, the most hated man in Lisbon.

He at once embarked on a programme of reform. Despite all opposition, something was achieved. The budgetary deficit, which for years had been steadily increasing, was diminished, and a relatively honest administration brought the national finances into a more promising position than they had known for years. It was a dictatorship, in so far as the professional politicians had for the time being been thrust aside; but it was only a temporary dictatorship, since elections had been promised for the April of the following year, 1908. And "all those whose interests were menaced by the proposed reforms, all the comfortable rotativists and political hypocrites, all those who wished to gain credit by themselves initiating the reforms, and hated them when coming from another, were united against Senhor Franco," wrote an English Liberal who was in Lisbon at the time. "Never have party passions so blinded all the politicians of a country to that country's interests as in the violent and, one may well add, cowardly attacks on Senhor Franco—it is scarcely surprising that he should have been obliged to resort to methods more arbitrary, which of course drew scandalised cries of rage from those who had made them necessary. . . . He had not begun by employing arbitrary methods. 'The Republican party,' wrote a Portuguese journalist, ' asked above all for liberty, and the first thing the Government of João Franco did was to give it liberty.

What was the result? The Republicans declared in the newspapers that they did not want the liberty given them by the Government.' "[2]

Franco was governing in the name of no party or clique, but in the name of Portugal; and the journals of Republican and Royalist, of Regenerador and Progressista alike, were united, for once, in opposition to him. But opposition more formidable than mere newspaper abuse was being marshalled to crush this new concept of government as a public service. The Grand Master of the Portuguese Grand Orient, Dr. Magalhaës Lima, went abroad to discuss with the heads of international Freemasonry what was to be done. An address delivered by him at the Cosmos Lodge in Paris on November 19, 1907, appeared on the agenda paper in these terms: "Portugal—decay of the Monarchy, necessity of a Republicanism—the future of the Republic." He was engaged in his diplomatic mission until the end of the year; all in touch with Masonry knew what was afoot. On December 25th there appeared in the *Bulletin* of the *Association anti-maçonnique de France* a prediction by the Abbé Tourmentin that the overthrow of King Carlos was imminent. Five weeks later, on February 1, 1908, the King, together with his eldest son, Dom Luis, was shot dead in the streets of Lisbon. Five years later the political gang who called themselves the "Democrats" erected a mausoleum in Lisbon in honour of Buiça and Costa, the men of the Carbonarios who did the deed.

The brief reign of the young King Manoel opened with the dismissal of Franco by Queen Amelia, who had seen her husband shot down, and knew to what he owed his death. "The Constitutional Monarchy, now more constitutional and less of a monarchy than ever, could offer the nation nothing but empty promises," wrote Sir George Young, Secretary to the British Legation at Lisbon. "The Cortès at once relapsed into the frenzy of faction that has nullified its function ever since the end of the old routine rotativism in 1906. No faction had any public force behind it, and no coalition of factions had any consistency, so that ministries followed one another at intervals of one or two months, or even weeks."[3]

Plans for the proclamation of the Republic proceeded rapidly, under the inspiration of some few who genuinely thought that therein lay the solution to the country's difficulties, and of Masonry, which wished thereby to gather control of the country solely to itself. Dr. Magalhaës Lima went again on a diplomatic tour in September 1910, conferring with the heads of Masonry in Brussels, Paris, and Madrid. In the first days of October the Revolution took place; the House of Braganza went into exile, and Portugal became a Republic. "It was a thunderbolt for the non-instructed public," said M. Furnemont, Grand Orator of the Belgian Grand Orient. "But we, my brethren, we knew. . . . We had the secret of this glorious event." "The work of the Portuguese Revolution is due exclusively to Masonry," wrote Machado Santos, the young lieutenant who had led it after the unfortunate suicide of Admiral Candido dos Reis, on page 34 of the Report which he published in 1911. It was not a true boast, but it was very nearly true.

It is not to be denied that the Monarchy was effete; it is not to be maintained that all Republicans were dishonest men. But it is to be maintained that that gang of Masonic Republicans that made the Portuguese Republic in 1910 made it to secure a hegemony for themselves. I am aware that to attribute all the evils of this time to Freemasonry is as absurd as the attribution by anti-clericals of all evils to the Jesuits. But I am also aware that few English readers have any idea of the part that is played and has been played in the past in continental politics by international Freemasonry, which seeks to reserve all power to itself and to crush the Catholic Church, and which in thus seeking to exclude its opponents from government and to impede the practice of the Faith of Europe represents the very negation of democracy. Those who wish for a fuller account of Masonic intervention will find it, fully documented, in *Le Portugal Renaît*,[4] by the Vicomte Léon de Poncins. In particular, they will find in the appendix to that work, supported throughout by quotation from Masonic documents, a detailed exposition of the way in which the Lusitanian Grand Orient has aspired to the domination of the Portuguese Republic.

In 1910, then, that Masonic gang among the Republicans who chose to call themselves "Democrats" were installed in power. They called themselves democrats, but they were at once involved in conflict with organisations of the working classes. "In 1911, the difficult first year of the Republic, Lisbon was threatened with a general strike, and local strikes were epidemic everywhere. In January 1912, a revolutionary strike in Lisbon was only quelled by the declaration of martial law and the arrest of over a thousand syndicalists."[5] And so on: nothing like it had been known before. They called themselves democrats, but they at once began a systematic and rigorous persecution of the religion of the poor. The first act of the Republic, in 1910, was to expel all the religious orders and to confiscate their property. In 1911 a lengthy decree was promulgated, giving detailed directions regarding the persecution of the Church and the penalisation of religion. Church property was confiscated, and in 1912 the Archbishops of Portalegre and Braga were expelled from the country. The family was attacked by the secularisation of marriage and the institution of divorce. They called themselves democrats, but they maintained themselves in power by the terror of the Carbonarios and by the cult of the bomb, extolled as the instrument of liberty.

The record of the Republic between 1910 and 1926 may thus be summarised in figures: during those sixteen years there were eight Presidents of the Republic (although by the 1911 Constitution the President was to be elected for four years); and there were forty-three different Ministries (although by the 1911 Constitution elections were to take place every three years, or five times during that period, so that these changes of government were not even in appearance connected with the people). The first Government of the Republic did not last ten weeks; the longest lasted little over a year. Revolution in Portugal became a by-word in Europe. The nation's finances passed from a condition which, although bad, seemed redeemable, to one which in 1927 was apparently hopeless. Budgetary deficits reached appalling figures, and periodical borrowings to cope with them sent the national debt to an amount equally appalling. The cost of living increased twenty-five fold, and the currency fell to one thirty-third part of its gold value. Before Portugal left the gold standard, in 1891, the exchange value of the Escudo (which is the Portuguese monetary unit) was 4.5 to the pound. In 1913 the rate of exchange was still 5.25 to the pound. But in 1925 the average rate was 131.563 to the pound.

It is true that the Great War had intervened; but the Great War might have seen the rehabilitation instead of the further collapse of the national finances, since it brought to the national credit the financial backing of the City of London. A vice-governor of the Bank of Portugal has emphasised: "Unlike those of most other nations, the resources of Portugal were not unduly taxed by the War—the crisis came from what may be called the spirit of the War—that is to say, the spirit of makeshift, of laxity, of squandering, of disorder."[6] A chief cause of the national bankruptcy was an inadequate revenue due to under-taxation and corrupt exemption under the Republic.

The financial question will be summarised later: the only point to be made here is that the nation was administered before Salazar in the very short-sighted interests of an oligarchy. We have noted the episode of João Franco, who challenged the oligarchy. There were two further challenges made before it was crushed by the national rising of 1926: those of General Pimenta de Castro and President Sidonio Paës.

In January 1915, a military *pronunciamiento* led to the overthrow of the seventh Government of the

Republic and gave power to General Pimenta de Castro. Lest this brief factual summary be taken for mere pamphleteer advocacy of authoritarianism we will quote again from Mr. A. F. G. Bell, who is a Librarian of the British Museum, and than whom no living Englishman has a more intimate knowledge of Portugal. "There was a general breath of relief throughout the country, and by an odd paradox this new Government born of a military movement, this 'dictatorship', this 'tyranny', proved the most moderate Government that Portugal had seen since the Revolution of 1910. With equal moderation and firmness one measure after another was enacted in order to bring about the long-dreamt reconciliation of all Portuguese. Churches were restored to the use of the faithful, officials arbitrarily dismissed were restored to their posts, the 'White Ants' were sent about their business, their so-called 'Committee of Public Safety' abolished, and finally in April a general amnesty emptied the prisons and allowed the eleven exiles of the 1914 amnesty to return to Portugal. O but, say the Democrats, it was all so unconstitutional! Such a dictatorship! Of course it was unconstitutional. The Constitution has been so ordered (Mr. Bell is writing in June 1915) that the Democrats having installed themselves in power— and they had been in power in fact if not in name since the Revolution—could never be dislodged by constitutional means. Their majority in the Chamber of Deputies was secure, their majorities in the town councils throughout the country, and in the officials responsible for returning the new deputies, equally secure. It became necessary to dissolve these bodies, by force if they would not go willingly. But the country which had suffered from four years of constitutional tyranny was delighted to have a little unconstitutional moderation. In vain the Democrats cried out that it was a dictatorship worse than the dictatorship of João Franco. If, answered common-sense opinion, the Government which empties the prisons, maintains order, and acts in every respect so fairly and moderately, is a dictatorship, then may all succeeding Governments be tarred with the dicta-torial brush. Only so will the future of the Republic and of Portugal be secure."[7]

Mr. Bell is, I repeat, an Englishman and a Liberal; he is not a political controversialist, but a distin-guished man of letters who has lived all his life in Portugal. He wrote this judgment on Pimenta de Castro at Estoril, a few miles outside Lisbon, in June 1915, before the words " Fascist " and " Nazi " had been invented. He knew exactly what he was writing about, and exactly what Liberal Democracy means and always has meant in the Iberian Peninsula: he knew exactly the value of that Portuguese political party which called itself " Democrat ", which, in May 1915, engineered mutiny in the army and the navy in order to displace Pimenta de Castro and restore itself to power. " The Democrat party," he wrote, " will always be known as the party which, under cover of the World War, raised itself to power over the dead bodies of its fellow countrymen."[7]

Sidonio Paës became President of the Portuguese Republic on May 9, 1917, a fortnight after Affonso Costa had become Prime Minister for the third time. Paës (whose name means " the country ") was a man with a great popular following and a strong patriotic sense; as Franco and de Castro had done, he challenged that political hegemony which Affonso Costa represented. That meant that he would be attacked and attacked again. He was also an ex-Mason (his name in the Lodges had been brother Carlyle). That meant death. For seven months he tried to work through the 1911 Constitution: it was not possible, least of all with Dr. Affonso Costa at the head of the Government. On December 5th he turned out the Government and proclaimed a dictatorship. It should be remembered that in these days before Mussolini and Hitler the word "dictatorship" was still used in the sense in which the Romans used it: it meant the temporary concentration of power in one man in time of national necessity. The dictatorship of Sidonio Paës had the support of the people; it also had the support of the army, which, being a cross-section of the people and relatively immune from political browbeating, is nearly always in Spain and Portugal the truest indication of national opinion. Affonso Costa was imprisoned: if the President had been in danger of assassination before, he was certain of it now. "Acclaimed by the crowd, he enjoyed a great popularity in the eyes of the masses of the country, which quickly felt the happy results of his good administration."[8] In a Latin and Catholic country like Portugal, the treatment of religion always provides a sure indication of the extent to which a Government is genuinely popular and democratic. Sidonio Paës gave justice to the Church which had been so relentlessly persecuted by the anti-clerical Masonry of the Republic. Diplomatic relations with the Vatican were restored; the Cardinal-Archbishop was allowed to return to Lisbon. But the rule of Sidonio Paës lasted only a year. At midnight on the night of December 14, 1918, he was murdered by a hireling of the Freemasons on the platform of the main station at Lisbon,[9] and Portugal fell back into confusion for another eight years.

From 1919 to 1926 the succession of "Governments" became even more rapid and bewildering. Terrorism and political assassination became general. Three hundred and twenty-five bombs burst in the streets of Lisbon (according to official police figures) between 1920 and 1925; the bloodiest night was that of October 19, 1921, when the Prime Minister, António Joaquim Granjo, met his death, with many others. The affairs of the country were in complete disorder. It became increasingly difficult to borrow to pay interest due on previous debts. And beneath the surface of chaos in public affairs, the people became more and more restless. The rule of the Republic was anarchy; the freedom of the Freemasons was terror. It was against this that the nation rose in May 1926.

II

THE MAN FROM NOWHERE

The Nation rose in May 1926: it was again the army that gave expression to the anger and despair of the people. On May 27th a brief manifesto, signed by the veteran Marshal Gomez da Costa, who had led the Portuguese Expeditionary Force to Flanders in the Great War, appeared on the walls of the garrison city of Braga:

> "For men of dignity and honour the political condition of the country is intolerable.
> Portugal: to arms, for the liberty and honour of the Nation!"

On the following day, a day which has become famous in the history of Portugal, men of every political opinion, Republican and Royalist alike, followed the army in a march on Lisbon: it was a march of patriots against the oligarchy. It was a march from the north, from the capital of the ancient Kings, from the first Kingdom of Portugal from which Lisbon and the south had been wrested eight centuries before from the Moors.

The Government, the sixth of António da Silva, resigned on May 30th; on the 31st the President of the Republic, Bernardino Machado, apostle of the bomb, renounced his charge in a letter to Commander Mendez Cabeçadas, leader of the revolution in Lisbon, who took power into his own hands until Marshal da Costa formally entered the city at the head of the army on June 17th. Shortly afterwards, da Costa, feeling that his work was done, made over the leadership to General Oscar Carmona: it is to these three men, da Costa, Carmona, and Cabeçadas, that the revolution that was to end revolution is due. Not a shot had been fired. By the middle of June the drift of a nation to disaster had been arrested.

A brief proclamation, signed by Marshal da Costa, told what was the purpose of the *coup d'état*:

"The Nation desires a National Government, composed of its most able citizens, to bring back to the administration of the State its lost discipline and honour.

"The Nation has had enough of the tyranny of irresponsible politicians. It wants a strong Government, whose object shall be the saving of the country and the institution of a real representation of the genuine, living, and permanent interests of Portugal.

"United with you in the hope of the redemption of our country, I proclaim the National interest against the fatal sway of politicians and parties, and I offer to the tormented country a strong Government, capable of presenting a brave face to internal and external foes."

The military Junta was rapidly able to establish public order. But in the matter of constructive politics the gallant soldiers had no very precise ideas. Da Costa was rather vague in his diagnosis of the situation : he was a soldier and no politician, but he had professed Liberalism all his life, and was not able to understand that Liberalism as known in Portugal was responsible for the sad situation against which he had led the army. Carmona was a man of longer vision who asked for radical reform, and not only reform, but re-formation of the political structure of the nation. He knew that if that were not forthcoming the military *coup d'état* of 1926 would be of no more ultimate effect than had been those of 1915 and 1917.

Fortunately for Portugal, his urgency prevailed and Marshal da Costa withdrew in his favour.

The most immediate and pressing necessity was to find a man capable of taking charge of the nation's finances. The soldier who was first given responsibility for that department called together the various officials of his Ministry and (so the story goes) announced to them: "I know absolutely nothing about finances myself, except that my own are in complete disorder." So were those of the nation: and the restoration of some sort of order to them—an apparently hopeless task—was necessarily the first step to be taken in any work of national reconstruction. It was decided that the best thing to do was to approach the Professor of Political Economy in the University of Coimbra. The Professor reluctantly agreed to undertake the work: he arrived at his Ministry on Friday, June 4, 1926. On the following Thursday, finding that he was required to work circumscribed by restrictions which made work impossible, he took the train back to Coimbra. He would not, and could not, assume responsibility unless he were given absolute discretion. The Ministry was then given to General Sinel de Cordes, who was quite unequal to the situation. In the autumn of 1927 it was decided that there was no alternative but to apply to the Financial Committee of the League of Nations for a loan such as had been granted through it to Austria, Hungary, Bulgaria, and other countries whose recovery from the War would otherwise have been impossible. The sum of £12,000,000 was required as being necessary for financial reconstruction and monetary stabilisation.

A League Commission visited Portugal and reported favourably; the loan should be granted, but its administration should be left in the hands of the League of Nations, which should also conduct an exhaustive preliminary inquiry into the financial condition of the nation and of the Bank of Portugal. These conditions were immediately rejected by the Government and by popular opinion alike. National sentiment had been roused by the recent revolution, and by the appeal to history of those responsible for it; and the humiliating proposal that the national administration should be subjected to international control was not considered for a day. The scorn of Senhor da Silva, of the Bank of Portugal, was typical: it was at Lisbon, he said, and not on the shores of an Alpine lake, that the crisis would be solved.

Meanwhile the Professor of Political Economy at Coimbra had been attracting some attention with a series of articles on the financial situation in the Catholic newspaper *As Novidades*. When the Geneva loan had been rejected, Carmona turned again to this man. His name was Dr. António de Oliveira Salazar. He had had some previous experience of politics, and at first when approached he refused to take office. Eventually he yielded, in response to an appeal to his sense of patriotic duty; but he only yielded on condition of being given absolute discretion, absolute power in his own sphere. If he was to be Minister of Finance, it was essential that he should be completely independent of any interested influence.

On April 27, 1928, he entered that Ministry for the second time. "I thank you," he said, addressing General Vicente de Freitas, the Premier, at a meeting of the Cabinet on that date, " for having decided, after discussion with the Cabinet, to entrust to me the port-folio of Finance, and also for the kind words which you have addressed to me. You must not thank me for having accepted this responsibility, for it repre-sents to me a sacrifice so great that I would not make it for any man merely in friendship. I make it for my country, simply as a duty dictated by my conscience." He then proceeded to enumerate the conditions on which alone he undertook the Ministry; they were accepted, and he holds that Ministry to this day, although he since assumed as well other and greater responsibilities.

It is apparent, therefore, that Salazar is not a man who fought his way to power, and that he accepted office as the nominee of no party or faction. He be-came a statesman reluctantly, and on his own terms. Always he longs for the academic quiet of his Univer-sity at Coimbra: by disposition he is a scholar, and even a recluse. He is the *homme d'état malgré lui*. Power is for him a heavy responsibility, an arduous public duty which he would greatly prefer to repu-diate; he professes himself willing at all times to return to Coimbra should it be wished. But too much depends on him. Practically alone he has set Por-tugal on her feet again. He has completely, and in-credibly, rehabilitated the national finances. It is always advisable to quote when making apparently wild statements, so we will quote *The Times*[10] to say that " it is impossible to deny that the economic im-provement recorded in Portugal since 1928 is not only without parallel anywhere else in the world, but is an achievement for which history can show but few precedents ". Moreover, there has been no repudiation of obligations, no artificial devices, no short cuts to solvency. The Portuguese budget has shown a substantial surplus every year since 1928, although ordinary expenditure has always been met from revenue, without recourse to loans. The national credit stands high in foreign markets; the external floating debt has been completely paid off; the Escudo has been stabilised; the internal price-level has long been steady; industry prospers, and extensive public works have been undertaken. Taxation, although mostly indirect, is high, but at least it is equitable, which was not the case before. The underlying principle in all this has been, and is, the subordination of all things to the national interest. A multiplicity of superfluous but salaried offices has been swept away. Inaccessible in his room in the Finance Ministry, under obligation to no one and fearing none, Salazar has been the most relentless of administrators, and the most just. He is without doubt one of the greatest Finance Ministers of our time, and has been generally recognised as such by a world that is less ready to approve his achievements in other directions.

On July 5, 1932, he succeeded General Domingo de Oliveira as President of the Council of Ministers, and in this capacity he was chiefly responsible for the Constitution of 1933, and for the Corporative organisation of the Portuguese Republic that was then initiated. In the Portugal of Salazar we have something that is unique in Europe. We have a Corporative State that is untainted with any form of totalitarianism. Liberal individualism has been superseded, but freedom remains.

And the debt of Portugal to Salazar is the greater when it is remembered that had it not been for him Portugal to-day would almost undoubtedly be a Soviet Republic; that is, Portugal to-day would be dead. Had the military rising of 1926 effected nothing more than a temporary order, had Salazar not come from obscurity like Cincinnatus or St. Joan of Arc to save his country, to arrest the national drift, then the first Soviet offensive in Western Europe would have come quite certainly from both sides of the Iberian Peninsula simultaneously; the subjection of Spain would have been relentless and brief, and Europe might well by to-day have been in flames. That is conjecture; it may appear to be idle conjecture. But Europe, as well as Portugal, owes a great debt to Marshal da Costa, the man who in 1926 took the initiative; to General Carmona, the man who saw a vision; and to Oliveira Salazar, the man who (the phrase is that of Gonzague de Reynold) "carries his power as a Christian carries his Cross".

III

SALAZar

António de Oliveira Salazar was born in 1889 at Santa Comba Dão, a village in Upper Beira, between Coimbra and Vizeu. His father kept a little inn in the village; his mother was a peasant woman. Their son is a Portuguese of the Portuguese, schooled in a hard school, brought up in close contact with the realities of life and death, with daily knowledge of poverty and of Faith.

He was educated at the seminary at Vizeu, where he later taught; and he received the minor orders there before he decided that he was not called to the priesthood. At the age of twenty-one he left for the University of Coimbra, where six years later, after a distinguished academic progress, he was appointed to the chair of Political Economy. He held this chair for twelve years before he was called to the service of the State. "A Professor he was," says Gonzague de Reynold, "and a Professor he remains. He works at the affairs of State with the same rigorous method and the same objectivity that he brought to the preparation of his lectures, of his books, and of his studies. He does nothing without careful consideration. He will not be hurried or disturbed; he shields himself from the importunate. Being at heart a shy man, he appears as little as possible in public. Deliberately he has earned the reputation of being inaccessible. He does not cultivate popularity; he mistrusts it. Finally, he is fiercely independent, and withdraws the moment he perceives that anyone is seeking to override his judgment, to influence him, or to enlist his support. These are the characteristics of the intellectual."[11]

He has remained always the student, the Professor of Economics; but he has remained also the peasant. To-day, when he guides the destinies of Portugal, he spends his leisure on the holding at Santa Comba Dão where he was born, travelling between there and the capital as an ordinary citizen, and hearing unrecognised the gossip of himself in the train or street. He retains the frugality, the simplicity of needs, of the peasant. The room at the Ministry of Finance in which he works has thus been described by Antonio Ferro: " A nondescript settee bearing a few cushions, a pile of dossiers on a fragile table that seemed to be emulating the leaning tower of Pisa. Some shelves with books, and, if I remember rightly, only three adornments on the walls: the image of the Sacred Heart of Jesus, the famous sonnet of Plantin, ' Le bonheur de ce Monde ', and the sympathetic portrait of an aged woman. In the centre of this humble room, Salazar's chair, with its back to the window, and his desk, on which are two or three sets of documents which have just been examined, the work he has in hand. Salazar, who wears his overcoat while he works, to keep out the cold, is seated at the desk."[12]

As President of the Council and Minister of Finance, his salary—decided by himself—is 5,000 *Escudos* a month, or less than £550 a year; and he lives strictly within this figure, regulating his personal affairs as meticulously as he regulates those of Portugal. The story is told of an occasion on which he broke a leg in a fall on the stairs at the Ministry, and the injury, sustained in the course of his work, took some time to heal. It was proposed that the doctors' expenses should be met from public money. Salazar would not hear of it, and sold a field at Santa Comba Dão to meet the charge.

He has remained always a poor man: he has remained also the man who had thought to become a priest. He is profoundly Catholic, and comes of a profoundly Catholic stock. "In some ways," says Gonzague de Reynold, "he reminds me of Mgr Ignace Seipel, Chancellor of Austria, and even of Cardinal Mercier." At the University of Coimbra he was the leading member of a little group engaged in studying social questions in the light of the encyclicals of Leo XIII, and of the work of the French Catholic sociologists, Le Play and de Mun and de la Tour du Pin. His politics have always been governed by Catholic principles. The great encyclical *Quadragesimo Anno* of Pius XI was published in 1931, and it it easy to trace the influence which it had on the new Portuguese Constitution upon which Salazar was at that time engaged, and which was promulgated two years later.

As a young man at Coimbra, he was attracted by a movement preaching "Integralismo Lusitano", a nationalist movement influenced by and analogous to the *Action Française* of Charles Maurras. He was interested in anything that gave promise of a national awakening, of a revival of the historic Latin and Christian Portugal, of a challenge to the existing social and political order, with its squabbling politicians and its down-trodden people. During the War he was concerned in the formation of the Catholic Centre Party, and wrote extensively on the need for reform in its newspaper, *As Novidades*; but his particular subject remained the study of economics and finance.

In 1921 he ventured for the first time into practical politics, and was elected to Congress; but he sat only for a single day, returning at once to Coimbra in disgust, to meditate on the wickedness of party politics. From then until 1926 the support which he gave to the Centre Party was intellectual alone. The story of his career may be continued in his own words. "I was and I am a simple Professor of Finance at the University of Coimbra. When the revolution of

May 28th broke out, the military committee at Lisbon came to offer me the portfolio of Finance, having the quite false idea that to Professors such as me all things are known. I refused the invitation for that reason, knowing the distance that separates the intellectual from the man of action. But they insisted so much that in the end I went to Lisbon, and interviewed General Gomez da Costa at Amadora. I excused myself on grounds of sickness and left for Santa Comba Dão, where, a few days later, they came to seek me; and I then became Minister for five days. At the re-shuffling of the Ministry I returned to Coimbra, together with some friends from the University who had also formed part of the Government. After the attempts of Commandant Filomeno da Camara and General Sinel de Cordes, they remembered me again, and here I am. It was Duarte Pacheco, at present Minister of Public Works, who this time came to Coimbra to fetch me in the name of the Government. As you see, the Catholics have always been strangers to my political career, to these successive voyages to and from Lisbon."[13]

That final sentence is important. Associated with the Catholic Centre Party, his accession to power had nothing to do with that association. When he came to power he diverted its activities into Catholic Action; he would have no more parties in Portugal. He will tolerate no cliques or factions of any kind whatsoever. A party in Portugal means not so much a way of approach to common problems as a gang, a camarilla, pursuing its own ends, and engaged in perpetual struggle with other parties, to the exclusion of all else. Salazar is influenced by no sub-national interest, but is concerned solely in a work of integration, in a grand synthesis of all that is best in Portugal into a government that is genuinely Portuguese.

He is profoundly Catholic: so is Portugal. He has done all in his power to preserve spiritual values against the rising tide of materialism. He has built up a New State, the *Estado Novo,* on a foundation of Christian moral principles. The Portuguese Pavilion at the Paris Exhibition must have made this clear to millions of visitors. A writer in the French Dominican journal *Sept*[14] has described a visit to the Pavilion, and how he found there evidences of " un redressement économique, mais tout imprégné de spiritualisme ". "One feels," he continues, "that the Professor from the University of Coimbra is not merely ' mindful of spiritual values ', and that still less is he influenced by the myths of Race, of State, or of Class; one knows that he is Christian through and through, and that he governs a Christian people."

He is profoundly Catholic. He has ended anti-clerical persecution in Portugal; he has suppressed Masonry, of which possibly the chief characteristic was hatred of the Church. But he has equally refused to countenance clericalism. As a youth at Vizeu he had received the minor orders; as a young man at Coimbra he shared a room with a young priest, Manuel Cerejeira, who became Cardinal Patriarch of Lisbon about the same time as Salazar entered the service of the State. It might have been expected that the Government of Portugal would soon become (in the usual but offensive phrase) "priest-ridden". But nothing of the kind has happened. Salazar has kept Church and State quite apart; in that he has shown himself supremely wise. So will the Church thrive best. "I was astonished," says Gonzague de Reynold, "to find that the *Estado Novo* has so far done relatively little for the Church." Yet should she suffer persecution in Portugal again, it will be said that she controlled the wealth and destinies of the country. Should the *Estado Novo* be challenged, it will be said that it was priest-ridden. It is probable (although I have not yet been able to confirm this) that the Government of Salazar has already been set down by the Liberals as a tyranny of the Romish Church.

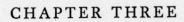

CHAPTER THREE

CHAPTER THREE

PRINCIPLES AND PRACTICE OF THE CORPORATE STATE

I

THE Portuguese State is defined by Article V of the Constitution of March 1933, as " a unitary and corporative Republic, founded on the equality of its citizens before the law, on the free access of all classes to the benefits of civilisation, and on the participation of all the elements that make up the nation in the administrative life and in the enactment of its laws ". The word " Corporative " means that the nation is regarded as an organic whole, and not as an accidental agglomeration of individuals; that it is organised by means of " Corporations ", or bodies representing the different phases of its life; and that these Corporations, together with the other associations that men may have formed for various purposes, since man is a social animal, are made the basis of the political and administrative life of the country. By Article XVI,[1] " It shall be the duty of the State to authorise, unless prevented by existing legislation, all corporative organisations, for intellectual, social, and economic purposes, and to encourage and to assist in their formation."

This corporative organisation has two aspects: the economic and social, and the political. It disciplines the national activity in a common harmony of interests, providing machinery for securing equal justice for all concerned therein; and, considered politically, it provides for the nation a form of government which can best be described as an organic democracy. Under both these aspects it lays emphasis on the Rights of Man (although in that matter it has masters other than the prophets of the French Revolution); but it lays equal emphasis on what are conceived to be the duties of man.

In the present chapter the economic and social aspects of the Corporate State in Portugal will be discussed. The chief documents that will be considered, as defining principles, are the Constitution of March 1933, and a series of Decree-Laws dated September 23rd of the same year. Of these latter, the first, known as the Statute of National Labour, which codifies what are taken to be the fundamental rights and duties of property, capital, and labour, and which defines the part to be played by the State in regulating the national economy, is very much the most important. This document is undoubtedly modelled on the Italian Charter of Labour of 1927; and the fact that there are many, if superficial, points of similarity between the Italian and Portuguese régimes makes it the more important that the distinctions should be emphasised. That is done in a later chapter: for the present, they can be summarised by saying that Fascism is something Italian whereas the *Estado Novo* is Portuguese, and that although Italy is a Corporate State, the corporatism of Italian Fascism is (in the French phrase for which there is no adequate translation) a *corporatisme d'état*, while Dr. Salazar has rejected *étatisme* in all its forms.

If it cannot be denied that Salazar owes a certain debt to Mussolini, it is very apparent that his greatest debt is to the social teaching of the Catholic Church. In particular the encyclical *Quadragesimo Anno*, published in May 1931, will be found to have had a profound influence on the Constitution which was drawn up by Salazar for his country during the following eighteen months and approved by a national plebiscite on March 19, 1933. This influence is so considerable that, purely as a matter of history, parallel phrases will be cited from the two documents. It is not proposed to make the papal encyclicals the sole criterion of excellence for the work of Salazar; the present brief study is not intended solely or even primarily for Catholics. But no account of him would be accurate that did not recognise the extent to which his ideas are derived from Catholic teaching.

After a consideration of the principles and theory that are embodied in the Portuguese Constitution and subsequent laws, we will proceed to a summary of what has already been achieved towards their realisation.

Article VI of the Constitution runs as follows:

" It is the duty of the State:

(1) To promote the unity of the Nation, and to establish order according to law, by defining and enforcing the rights and guarantees that

63

derive from morals, equity, or law, for the benefit of the individual, the family, the local authority, and other corporate bodies, both public and
private.

(2) To co-ordinate, stimulate, and direct all social
activities so that a just harmony of interests may
prevail, taking account of the legitimate subordination of private interests to the general
well-being.

(3) To strive for improvement in the condition of
the least favoured classes of society, and to
prevent their standard of life from falling below
the minimum necessary to human subsistence."

Here is a citation from the Constitution, with its
primary reference to the moral law, and its primary
concern for the poor, that cannot fail to recall the
encyclicals. The function of the State is defined as
"to co-ordinate, stimulate, and direct"; whereas
Quadragesimo Anno used the words "directing,
watching, stimulating, restraining, as circumstances
suggest and necessity demands".[2]

The point is expanded in Article VII of the Statute
of National Labour, and in Article XXXI of the Constitution, of which the text is as follows:

"The State has the right and the obligation to supervise the co-ordination and control of economic and
social life with the following objects:

(1) To establish a proper balance in the population,
the professions, occupations, capital, and labour.

(2) To protect the national economy against agricultural, industrial, and commercial ventures of a parasitic nature, or of a character incompatible with the higher interests of human life.

(3) To ensure the lowest prices and the highest wages that are consistent with the just remuneration of the other factors of production, by means of the improvement of technique, public services, and the national credit.

(4) To develop settlement in the national territories, to protect emigrants, and regulate emigration."

And Article XXXIV:

"The State shall encourage the formation and the development of the national corporate economy. It shall guard carefully lest the elements which comprise it tend to establish among themselves an unrestricted competition such as is contrary to the just ends of society and of themselves, but that they rather are encouraged to collaborate with one another as members of the same collectivity."

The function of the State as here defined corresponds exactly to that given to it by the Pope, who insists that " all the occupational groups (which make up a nation) should be fused into an harmonious unity, inspired by the principle of the common good. And the genuine and chief function of public and civil authority consists precisely in the efficacious furthering of this harmony and co-ordination of all social forces."[3]

It is further laid down by the Statute of National Labour that "the State should abjure all industrial or commercial exploitation, whether in the form of competition with private enterprises in the economic sphere, or in the form of monopoly, even if the result of such enterprises is designed, wholly or in part, to be used for public services. It shall only be able to establish or carry on exploitations of this kind in exceptional cases, and to obtain social advantages superior to those which would be obtained otherwise. Similarly, the State cannot take a direct part in the administration of private enterprises unless it is called upon to finance them in order to obtain such results" (Article VI: cp. also the Constitution, Art. XXXIII). "The State recognises in private initiative the most fruitful instrument of progress and of national economy" (Article IV). "The State recognises the right of ownership, and the powers of using and disposing of property that follow therefrom, as a rational necessity deduced from the nature of man, as leading to the greatest individual and collective effort in the family and in society, and as one of the first bases of social conservation and progress" (Article XII).

Private ownership is a fundamental fact in the Portugal of Salazar. The right to own is one of the chief of the rights of man as there conceived; it is defined as fundamental at the beginning of the Constitution, together with freedom of thought and of meeting and association, and other rights upon which Liberal constitutions lay exclusive emphasis (Article VIII, 15; see note 5, p. 155, below). It is a right that has been denied equally by Capitalism and by Socialism, which is the logical conclusion of Capitalism. Capitalism means the concentration of ownership in the hands of a few, and therefore denies men the natural right of ownership; Socialism seeks to remedy the state of affairs so produced by withdrawing ownership even from the few. Salazar would restore ownership to many.

It is a necessary principle; and, Salazar has said, "If we are obsessed exclusively by the idea of wealth, of production, we cannot be either for or against the large or the small owner: we must favour the one here and the other there, according to geographical, climatic, and economic conditions. But—and this is my point—if we do not reduce the life of society to terms of the production and the utilisation of wealth; if we find that that aspect of life, however necessary, should be tempered, completed or corrected by other realities—such as tranquillity, happiness, well-being, and the beauty of family life—then we can laugh at the cut-and-dried formulas for higher productivity, and decide at once for a policy of breaking up the great rural estates, and of systematically making small-holdings in which peasant families can be established in their ownership.

"Such a policy is an essential part of my ideas; but it conflicts, on the other hand, with the principles of those who materialise life, and regard man, as do the Russians, as a machine for producing and consuming wealth. So you see that the proper interest of States, and above all of the so-called Capitalist States, is to create the largest possible number of small proprietors, who, far from assisting communism and socialism, will become a solid conservative foundation for the Nation, and will oppose to the last all libertarian ideas."[4]

Salazar goes on to describe what steps have been taken and are being taken to carry out this policy of encouraging the small proprietor; let it be noted that they do not include expropriation of the rich. Three-fifths of the Portuguese are engaged in agricultural work, and this large-scale policy in favour of small farmers at once characterises the new régime. It is popular. If the English reader finds it difficult to understand unless it is assimilated to some -*ism* that is known to him, it is much more nearly true to say of the Portugal of Salazar that it is a Distributist State than to say that it is Fascist. But it is better to keep -*isms* out of the matter altogether, more especially as so many, just as they associate Fascism vaguely with castor-oil and concentration-camps, think only of Distributism—if they think of it at all—in connection with beer and the cult of the homespun.

The work that has been done in Portugal towards the creation of an independent and owning peasantry will be referred to in the fourth section of this chapter. But it is not only in agriculture that the small man is encouraged and protected. In pursuance of its duty of "co-ordinating, stimulating, and directing", the State, by Article XXXII of the Constitution, must "encourage those private economic activities which are most profitable in proportion to their costs, but without prejudice to the social benefit conferred by small home industries, or to the protection which is due to them". It is rarely that "the social benefit conferred by small home industries" has received constitutional recognition.

The whole of Section III of the first part of the Constitution concerns the position of the Family in the *Estado Novo*. Article XII enumerates the claims of the family to the protection of the State: "The State shall ensure the constitution and protection of the family, as the source of preservation and development of the race, as the first basis of education and of social discipline and harmony, and as a fundamental of political and administrative order, by its association in the parish (*freguesia*) and in the municipality, as well as by its representation in the local authorities governing these." That is, the moral importance of the institution of the family is recognised equally as its merely physiological importance as "the source of the preservation and development of the race". It is "the first basis of education and of social discipline and harmony". "To our knowledge," says Senhor Pereira dos Santos, in his exhaustive treatise on the Portuguese Constitution, "there is no other constitutional text on the rôle of the family in the State that is so comprehensive as this. . . . Generally, it is only its physiological function that is cited as the sole reason that justifies the protection of the family by the public authority."[5] He refers those who doubt to no less than six modern constitutions; but he was writing, of course, before the publication of the remarkable new Constitution of Eire.[6]

Article XIV of the Portuguese Constitution is this:

"With the object of protecting the Family, it appertains to the State and to local authorities:

(1) To encourage the establishment of separate homes under healthy conditions, and the institution of the family household.

(2) To protect maternity.

(3) To establish taxation in accordance with the legitimate expenses of the family, and to promote the adoption of the family wage.

(4) To assist parents in the discharge of their duty of instructing and educating their children, and to co-operate with them by means of public institutions for education and correction, or by encouraging private establishments destined for the same purpose.

(5) To take all effective precautions to guard against the corruption of morals."

The third and fourth clauses here seem of particular significance. The family wage is but an extension of the principle of the living wage. "Remuneration ought not to be insufficient to support a frugal and well behaved wage-earner," says *Rerum Novarum*. "There is, by principle, a minimum of wage or salary which corresponds to the needs of existence," says the Portuguese Statute of National Labour. But to define constitutionally that taxation must consider pre-eminently the necessity of providing the *family* with adequate means of subsistence is an excellent application of the principle that the State exists for society, and not society for the State.

The fourth clause of the above article, however, is

the most remarkable. The family, and not the State-owned and compulsory school, is the natural milieu of the child. The first right of parents is the right of caring for their own children, and it is a right which in Portugal is recognised. In England it is increasingly denied. Elementary and secondary schools, and technical colleges, are maintained in Portugal by the State, and every child is bound to receive at least an elementary education. But every parent is free to decide whether his child shall receive that education at home, in a private school, or in a State school; and the home is considered to be the normal place. Freedom of education is another of those liberties guaranteed by the Constitution under Article VIII; and it is a liberty which in England is not enjoyed.

" The State," says Salazar, " is not in Portugal the chief educator; the educative function lies primarily with the family, with which the State collaborates, only substituting itself when the family does not exist, or when it is unable to undertake its proper function."

The family, then, is the primary social unit; and, moreover, the independent, *owning*, family. We will again sum the matter up in the words of Salazar. "The family which dwells beneath its own roof is necessarily more thrifty, more stable, better constituted. That is why great blocks of flats, colossal houses for the workers, with their adjoining restaurants and their common table, do not interest us. All that is all right for the chance encounters of life, for the already semi-nomadic populations of our great contemporary civilisation; for our independent nature and simpler tastes, we prefer the small independent house, inhabited by the family which owns it."[7]

II

Two important points must be seized from the foregoing brief summary of Salazar's conception of society and of the functions and position of the State. The first characterises his work throughout: it is his constant and primary deference to the natural and moral law, and his basic acceptance of Christian concepts of the nature of man and of society. It is made abundantly clear in his speeches. "Apart altogether from the intrinsic value of religious truth to the individual and society, we have need of an absolute; and we are not going to create that which exists outside and above us with our own hands. We are not going to arrogate to the State the function of decreeing belief, of defining the principles of moral law. We are led, therefore, to consider Power as morally limited, and we have sought to avoid the error or the crime of deifying the State, or Force, or Riches, or Beauty, or Vice—we do not challenge God."[8]

It is the moral law which is first acknowledged by the Portuguese Constitution.[9] Man's right to own property is "deduced from the nature of man", as St. Thomas Aquinas deduced it. It is so throughout the legal documents which embody the principles of the *Estado Novo*. The work of Salazar has been to achieve a Christian and traditionalist re-awakening. "Certes, il y a d'abord un but économique," writes Gonzague de Reynold, "puis un but social, puis un but national; mais, plus haut, au fond de l'avenue, comme la statue où aboutissent toutes les lignes de la

perspective, il y a le but moral. Le régime corpora-
tiste est nettement spiritualiste."

The second point, which must be emphasised
before we proceed to discuss the practical details of
the Portuguese Corporate State, is that it is to be so
far as is possible a spontaneous development. The
duty of the State, as has already been said, is to " encourage ": to " co-ordinate, stimulate, and direct " the
corporative organisation; it is not the duty of the
State itself to create, or to impose from above. In
the words of Article XVI of the Constitution, which
we have already quoted (p. 61), the State must
" authorise ": that is, it does not normally take the
first step. Its rôle consists essentially in making good
the shortcomings of spontaneous initiative, of comple-
menting individual effort. This function has never
been exceeded; if it be thought that at times rather
a large degree of State assistance has been required
to complement individual effort, it should be remembered what manner of people are the Portuguese.

They will never do to-day what can possibly be done
to-morrow: it is *mañana, mañana*, as with the Spanish.
They are a strange, sad, melancholy people, characterised by the *saudade*, the feeling that their days of
greatness are past, that they have fallen and cannot
get up again, that there is nothing for it but to sing
and to wait for to-morrow, *mañana*, when they will
be great again. But it is always *mañana*.

It is an indolence inherited of centuries against
which the Government of Salazar has to work. Nevertheless, the State has reduced its own obtrusiveness to
a minimum. It has abjured bureaucracy. The fifth
clause of Article VII of the Statute of National Labour

says: "The State shall reduce to the indispensable minimum the sphere of action of its officials in the national economy." Again, the preamble to the Decree-Law of July 8, 1936, declares that the Corporate State can only live if it is administered through organs as far as possible removed from the Portuguese equivalent of Whitehall, and as nearly as possible in contact with the different members of the corporate body; and it goes on to provide for the institution by the Minister of Commerce and Industry, of bodies "designed to co-ordinate, and, in the last resort, to regulate economic and social life in those professions which are directly concerned in export and import": that is, to supervise and ensure that "just harmony of interests" and the "legitimate subordination of private interest to the general well-being" of which the Constitution speaks. "These bodies," says Fr. Muller, the distinguished Belgian student of corporative theory, "will serve both as instruments for the exercise of State supervision and as a means of giving to the Corporations a degree of autonomy. Their composition is designed to bring the representatives of the State and of the interests concerned into direct collaboration. It is a new idea, not to be paralleled in any other corporative régime, and illustrates the desire of the Portuguese 'dictatorship' to reduce State intervention to a minimum, and, even in the exercise of the most necessary control, to leave as much as is possible to priviate initiative."[10]

The ultimate ideal is that the Corporations representing the various industrial and commercial activities of the nation shall be entirely autonomous. "The State," writes Salazar, "refrains from itself directing

the Corporation, and only reserves for itself the right
—which it regards as a duty—of ensuring that the law
is carried out, and that the interests of the community
are protected. To go further would, in its opinion,
not only be to complicate the task of government, but
to prejudice social life."[11]

This is a fact of the utmost importance, and is one
of the chief reasons why the corporatism of Portugal
is essentially different from Italian Fascism. Pius XI,
after briefly recapitulating Fascist theory, writes:
"Little reflection is required to perceive the advantages of the institution thus summarily described . . .
but . . . there are some who fear that the State is substituting itself in the place of private initiative, instead
of limiting itself to necessary and sufficient assistance.
It is feared that the new syndical and corporative
organisation tends to have an excessively bureaucratic
and political character."[12] This is the chief criticism
which, in 1931, he had to make of the Corporate State
of Italy. It does not apply to the Corporate State of
Portugal.

The Corporate State is a misleading term; it would
be better to refer to the Corporate Nation. There is
no *étatisme* in Portugal; and Salazar has repeatedly
declared that there shall not be. "During long con-
versations which I had the honour to have with
Senhor Teotonio Pereira, then Under-Secretary of
State for the Corporations, and with Salazar himself,"
again to quote Gonzague de Reynold, "both continu-
ally emphasised their strong opposition to *étatisme*.
That for which they wish, that for which they are
working, is a *corporatisme d'association*, and not a
corporatisme d'état."[13]

The Portuguese Corporate State is growing organically, like a plant; it is being tended from above, but
the seed from which it springs is deep in the soil of
Portugal. The historic Guild system survived in Portugal in a very real form until the nineteenth century,
and was only finally suppressed, in the name of
Liberalism, by a decree of May 7, 1834. A political
invasion accompanied the Napoleonic invasion of
Portugal: what Salazar has described as the "alien
and exotic plant" of Liberalism was obtruded on a
country exhausted by thirty years of invasion and
civil war. During the remainder of the nineteenth
century Portugal was dominated by alien influences,
and exploited to the full by English and German
capital. But the true and historic Portugal was not
dead, even if trampled underfoot; and as the century
wore on, and confusion became steadily worse confounded, she began to re-assert herself. The old Corporative ideal found more and more adherents as the
effects of political and economic Liberalism made
themselves apparent; and it received great stimulus
towards the end of the century from the publication
of the great social encyclical of Leo XIII, *Rerum
Novarum*. By the side of this revival of the ancient
theory of economic organisation came a strong movement for political nationalism. We have seen how
Salazar as a young man was associated with these
tendencies. His work in restoring the corporative
system to Portugal, seen in its historical perspective,
becomes but a vindication of the historic Portugal.
He has ended the long period of alien domination.

It would be absurd to pretend that the ancient Guild
system had not outlived its usefulness in 1834, just as

it would be absurd to press too far the analogy between the ancient Guild and the modern Corporation. But what I have written remains true: Salazar has restored Portugal to herself. He has realised a spontaneous and natural movement. That is partly what is meant by saying that the corporatism of the *Estado Novo* is a *corporatisme d'association*. What also is meant is that the corporate organisation is not imposed from above, but encouraged to develop from below, from the people, from the Nation.

It possesses a degree of adaptibility, of suppleness, which will be made clear as this discussion of it proceeds, and which is one of its chief strengths. It is not a system so much as a principle: the organisation of the nation is being modified to suit particular circumstances, shaped to local conditions. It is growing organically.

"Although we have not yet completely constituted a single Corporation," wrote Salazar in 1936, "the corporative spirit is beginning to penetrate the national economy, and that is essential for the success of the régime. Sometimes we have to make experiments with pre-corporative bodies before envisaging typically corporative organisation, to open the way, as it were, rather than run the risk of compromising an ideal by lack of preparation."[14] To M. de Reynold he said: "It is essential to go slowly in organising the Corporations, for it is first and foremost necessary to develop the corporative *spirit*, without which the Corporations must risk degenerating, either into a system of trusts, or into one of State bureaucracy. For the present, the State is forced into continual intervention, because it is coming into continual conflict with individualist opposition and with Portuguese apathy. We do not wish to introduce corporatism everywhere all at once; we are proceeding as we can, beginning at the beginning, and taking account of local circumstances."[15]

" One cannot but be astonished," writes Fr. Muller, " in studying the new corporative régime of Portugal, by the remarkable restraint shown in the legislative documents which are bringing it into being. The third section of the Statute of National Labour, devoted to the corporative organisation, is all contained in ten articles; the decree concerning the *gremios*, or employers' associations, has no more; the decree concerning the national syndicates is all compressed into twenty-five articles. The constitution and administration of the syndicates have alone been treated in some detail. We have scarcely any information about the organisation and internal administration of the employers' associations, and we know nothing at all about the Federations envisaged as intermediary in the corporative structure. On the Corporations themselves the Statute of National Labour provides only some very general principles.

" A bewildering brevity indeed, and a change from the cut-and-dried systems to which certain enthusiasts for the corporative idea have accustomed us. Such people like to display before our eyes the pieces of an ingenious mechanism which they have invented, to describe the unfailing precision of its various parts, to expatiate on the exact working and the precise balance of its strictly ordered organisations, apparently without being aware that society is organic, that life does not permit of prescribed rules for its development. Corporative organisation is not assembled like a machine; it is born, it grows and flourishes from the impulse of internal and spontaneous forces which the legislator can certainly 'direct, watch, stimulate, restrain', but on which it is useless for him to attempt to impose his will."[16]

Salazar is never afraid or reluctant to admit mistakes, to modify, to go back, to abandon any scheme which in practice proves unsatisfactory. But he will never abandon the fundamental principles to which in his speeches and writings he constantly returns. Perhaps one of the most important things about the Portuguese Corporate State is that it is still frankly experimental; and perhaps one of the most important things about Salazar is his dictum that "the State represents a doctrine in action". When first he took office he said : "I know exactly what I want and where I am going." He has proved that to be true. Even the Constitution of Portugal contains ample provision for revision. But in the fundamental principles on which the work of national reconstruction is based there can be no revision.

First among those principles is that Portugal shall be Portugal. For a century she has suffered the encroachments of English and German financial and commercial interests, and of French political and intellectual influences: the *francezismo*. We have made a general comparison between the Portuguese people and the Irish; and both in Portugal and in Ireland have the years since the Great War seen a revolt against alien domination, and the acceptance by the people of new Constitutions inspired by

79

Christian principles equally as by a spirit of national pride.

III

"We have distorted the idea of wealth; we have divorced it from its object, which is to serve worthily the life of man. We have put it into a separate category, apart from the interests of the community and apart from moral concepts; and we have imagined that the destiny of individuals, of States, and of nations, is to accumulate goods without regard for social utility, without regard for justice in their acquisition or their use.

"We have distorted the idea of labour, and we have forgotten the personality of the labourer, his dignity as a human being; we have thought only of his value as a producing machine, we have measured or weighed his productive power and we have not so much as remembered that he is a member of a family, that life is not in him alone, but in his wife, his children, and his home.

"We have gone further: we have dispersed his home. We have called forth the woman and the child as factors in production, less efficient but cheaper —as detached units, elements entirely independent of one another, without bonds, without affection, without a life in common; in fact, we have destroyed the family. At one stroke, we have broken into the family circle; and, having increased competition amongst the workers by introducing the labour of women, we have not accorded to each family in salaries the value of the industry of a good housewife, of the social usefulness of the mother of a family.

"We detached the worker from the natural surroundings of his profession: free from the bonds of association, he remained alone; without the discipline of the association, he became free, but defenceless. Next we allowed him to ally himself with others and he did so, by reaction, not in order to achieve unity, not with the aim of helping to co-ordinate all the various factors in the work of the production of wealth, but in *opposition* to someone or something—in opposition to the State, which is the guardian of order, in opposition to his employers, whom he regarded as a hostile class, even in opposition to other workers. . . . No objects of intellectual or moral advancement, or of the improvement of professional technique, or of insurance or provident work; no spirit of co-operation—nothing but hate, destructive hate.

"We forced the State, at first, into an absolute passivity, unconcerned, whether willingly or not, in the organisation of the national economy; and then into an all-absorbing intervention, which regulated the production, the consumption, and the distribution of wealth. . . . Those who, blindly driven by the logic of their false principles, have carried this to its conclusion, have mounted the machine with a great show of system, with the apparent infallibility of science and advanced technique; but the free worker, the MAN, has disappeared, caught up in the colossal mechanism that is without mercy and without mind. We have seen the workers mobilised like machines, shifted like cattle when the pasture fails."[17]

That is an indictment by Salazar of the Liberal inheritance. Society was disintegrated by Liberalism; Salazar seeks a solution by synthesis, by reconstruction, instead of by regimentation. He seeks to restore to society the groupings which are natural to man. A man lives first in his family, secondly in his trade. The family is to be protected and preserved. And men who work in different ways will form different professional associations, not so much for defence of their professional interests as to make possible their collaboration in the life of the community; and not more for that than for such purposes as the development of professional technique, the pursuance of common ideals, the protection of their fellows in times of adversity and misfortune. Employers will have their associations, and workers theirs. Wider organisations will co-ordinate into a Corporation all concerned in a given branch of activity; and the various Corporations will be co-ordinated in a Corporative Chamber, in which also national problems and public affairs will be discussed by those with particular knowledge of them.

"It is natural that just as those who dwell in close proximity constitute townships, so those who practise the same trade or profession, in the economic field or any other, form corporate groups." "In these corporations the common interests of the whole vocational group must predominate; and among these interests the most important is to promote as much as possible the contribution of each trade or profession to the common good."[18] These words might well be those of Salazar, but they are not.

The Corporations represent no more than the

different occupations in which men are engaged, organised so that they may adequately collaborate with the State in promoting the national well-being. For the Corporations are the component parts of the nation, considered functionally; and, since the nation is an entity, an organic whole, the interests of its component parts are ultimately identical with the national interest.

Each Corporation, each occupational group, is responsible for its own corporate life, as were the Medieval Guilds. It must protect all those engaged in the branch of activity with which it is concerned; it must see that they are adequately rewarded for their work, it must defend their rights, it must provide for them in times of misfortune.

It is, as we have already said, misleading to press the analogy with the medieval Guild system too far, but there is this in common : that society is regarded as being divided, as it were, vertically, according to trade or profession or occupation, instead of horizontally according to social status or (what is worse) according to income. It is an elementary principle that all idea of the class-war is to be repudiated. "The hierarchy of functions and social interests is an essential condition of the national economy,"[19] says the Statute of National Labour; and it should be seen at once that that is not inconsistent with the vertical division of society. So far as the Portuguese State is concerned, there are not upper, middle, and lower classes; but there are men concerned in the cork industry, men concerned in the wine industry, and so on. In each industry "the hierarchy of functions" must remain; there will be authority and obedience, but not absolute authority and wage-slavery. Strikes and lock-outs and all such methods of class defence are specifically declared illegal both by the Constitution and by the Statute of National Labour.[20] There are associations alike of employers and employed; but the first purpose of these is not to defend the interests of a class, but to collaborate in the interests of the community. That is why it is misleading to refer to the workers' associations as " Trade Unions ", with its implication of motives of defence; the word " syndicate " is also misleading, as it has different associations in different places; but the Portuguese use it, so we must do the same.

The Portuguese national syndicates, according to Article IX of the Decree-Law which governs them, " should subordinate their own interests to the interests of the national economy, in collaboration with the State and with the higher organs of production and of labour ". The key principle in all corporative theory is the principle of the common good.

The national syndicates group together the employees and wage-earners in a given industry; and their formation has from the start been left freely to the initiative of those concerned, although they must secure Government recognition, and, of course, not more than one syndicate will be recognised for each industry in the same neighbourhood. Their statutes, to receive approval and recognition, must expressly repudiate the class struggle, and declare readiness to co-operate with the other factors in the national economy. They do not vary much : the interests of the working-man are very much the same in all places. Whatever his trade and wherever he lives, he requires reasonable hours, reasonable conditions of work, an adequate wage, good housing, and so on. Consequently, the terms of the law governing the syndicates are much more precise than is possible for those concerning the employers' associations, which vary considerably.

Decree-Law No. 23,050 of September 23, 1933, lays down that ordinarily no syndicate containing fewer than a hundred members will be recognised; that not more than one syndicate for each trade may be formed in each district;* that the capital town of the district will normally be its headquarters; that membership will not be compulsory, but that juridical personality will be granted to the syndicates, which will legally represent all workers in its industry and district, whether members or not. Rules governing their organisation are also given. Part of the function of the syndicates is to negotiate collective labour contracts with the employers' associations; but they are also essentially concerned with the welfare of their members. Article XII imposes on them the obligation to set up syndical providential societies, to organise agencies for finding employment for workers in the trade with which they are concerned, and to establish and maintain schools for professional and technical instruction; and "some syndicates have built schools for their members' children, sanatoria and crèches, provided medical aid and medicines, and obtained good and cheap houses, out of those built by the State, for their members. Subsidies in sickness and unemployment have been provided. Technical

* The "District"—*Distrito*—is a Portuguese administrative area corresponding, roughly, to the English county.

classes, language courses, and general educational lectures have been given. . . . Many public meetings have been held, which have enabled employers and workers to meet in a friendly atmosphere."[21]

The employers' associations are known as *gremios*, and are practically all governed by Decree-Law No. 23,049, also of September 23, 1933. According to this law, the *gremios* are to be created by ministerial initiative; and we are confronted with what appears to be a species of *corporatisme d'état*. The greatest merit of this law is its elasticity; no uniform regulations are provided for the *gremios*, but each is to be adapted to the particular conditions of the industry with which it is concerned. And just as it is essential that particular circumstances should be allowed to modify and to vary the application of an ideal, so it must be remembered that immediate but temporary necessities must frequently compel deviation from what is in theory best. The apparent *corporatisme d'état* of the first law dealing with the employers' associations was partly a result of the conditions prevailing in the anarchy of the years before 1926, but, even more, it was a necessary result of that international disaster technically known as a "crisis", or "slump", which hit the world so soon after Salazar began his work.

Before the promulgation of the Constitution, some branches of production had actually appealed to the Government for some sort of organisation. In the sardine industry, for instance, which is one of the most important in Portugal, markets were being lost to foreign competition and honest firms were being hopelessly undercut by unscrupulous exporters of tins full of cheap but rancid fish. The victimised firms appealed to the Government, and Salazar, then only Minister of Finance (1931), carried out a thorough study of the industry and its problem, and issued a report. On the recommendation of this report, the production and export of sardines were strictly regulated, and a "Consortium of Sardine Canners" was created, of which membership was compulsory. This piece of State interference saved an extremely important industry from ruin at the hands of foreign and unscrupulous competitors. Similarly, order was introduced into the port wine industry by compelling the co-operation of all producers. The organisations then set up were "pre-corporative" in type, and have since been revised as the Corporate State develops.[22]

When the legislation of 1933 extended order and co-ordination to all forms of national activity, it is not, then, surprising to find that production was at first organised by the Government, to which production had itself appealed. But very soon we find a striking proof of the desire of the Government for a true *corporatisme d'association*, in the preamble to a second important Decree-Law about the *gremios*, that of December 3, 1934. This defends the previous law on grounds of necessity; and continues: "The organisation of employers, while conforming to the objects prescribed for it and the duties imposed upon it by corporative law, ought not normally to proceed from Government initiative, nor attempt compulsorily to include all enterprises. It will arise from the initiative of those who are themselves interested, who will have to furnish their own effort, assume their own responsibilities, study the problems which concern them most nearly, and enter into the rôle which falls to them under the corporate organisation."

This is more in keeping with the rest of Salazar's legislation. Groups that are optional and formed by, instead of compulsory and imposed on, the employers of labour, are now recognised by the Government. The only condition made is the necessary one that they shall include at least half of all those engaged in the industry in question, and shall represent at least half of the financial interest involved. Otherwise rival associations might spring up in competition, or minorities might secure recognition, and there would not be any true participation of that industry in the corporative structure. Such associations will receive full recognition; that is, they will be accorded juridical personality, and will legally represent all employers in the industry and district of their competence; and conditions of labour agreed upon by them in meetings with representatives of the workers' syndicates will be similarly binding on all, whether members or no. Steps taken by them for the benefit of the industry with which they are concerned shall be binding on all when sanctioned by the Government on the recommendation of the Corporative Council.

"Par l'orientation nouvelle qu'il vient de donner à sa politique corporative, le Gouvernement portugais adhère à la formule d'auto-discipline, en quoi nous voyons l'expression la plus sincère de l'idée corporative," comments Fr. Muller. "De grand cœur nous applaudissons à cette innovation, dont nous attendons, pour le progrès de l'organisation professionnelle au Portugal, les plus heureux résultats."[23]

It is perhaps misleading to refer to the *gremios* as
"employers' associations", since they are groupings
by function: a man belongs to a *gremio* as being a
producer, a contributor to the national wealth, rather
than as being an employer of labour. Nevertheless,
an essential purpose of the syndicates and the *gremios*
is that they should meet together to draw up collective
labour contracts, and to ensure good relations between
employers and employed. Disputes or differences
arising out of such collective bargaining come before independent tribunals, under the administrative
authority of the National Institute of Labour and
Social Welfare, against the decisions of which appeals
may be made, on points of law, to the Supreme Council of Public Administration.[24]

Both national syndicates and *gremio*s have a
consultative function, and must furnish advice and
information on matters of their competence when
required. They have also a political function, which
will be referred to in the following chapter.

The syndicates and *gremios* concerned in different
parts of the country in the same industry are grouped
into regional or national "Federations", and Federations concerned with allied industries or pursuits are
further co-ordinated in "Unions". And all these
various groupings are finally to be integrated into Corporations. "Being representative of the general interests of production, the Corporations can establish
among themselves general and binding rules dealing
with their internal discipline and the co-ordination of
activities, always providing that they shall have received the necessary powers from the syndicates or
gremios, Unions or Federations, which comprise

them, as well as the authorisation of the State." (Statute of National Labour: Art. XLIII.) It is important to remember that the Corporations are to be so far as possible autonomous, and that authority is to travel upwards, as it were, from the bottom, instead of downwards from the top. The Corporations came last into being: they represent the final work of integration. Let this be remembered by those who attempt too hasty a comparison with Italian Fascism.

The purposes of the Corporation, as of the syndicates and other corporate bodies, are not merely economic; any more than the purpose of the medieval Guild was merely economic. But they go further than did the Guilds in having a political function. The Corporative bodies take part in the election of the Municipal Chambers, the Provincial Councils, and the Corporative Chamber. The Chamber crowns the corporative organisation of the nation, bringing together representatives of all phases of national activity to discuss and resolve their common problems, and to shape all the nation's work towards national well-being and prosperity. This political aspect of corporatiom is the matter of the next chapter, in which the Corporative Chamber will be discussed in detail.

It remains here to mention two further bodies: the National Institute of Labour and Social Welfare, and the Corporative Council. The former, which is presided over by the Under-Secretary of State for the Corporations, exists in order " to ensure the fulfilment of the laws protecting the workers, and of other laws of social character, by integrating the workers, and others taking part in production, in the corporative organisation, as laid down in the Statute of National

Labour, according to the spirit of political, economic, and social renovation of the Portuguese Nation ".[25]

The Corporative Council is the supreme body through which is exercised the general supervision of the Government over the development of the corporate structure. According to the law establishing it,[26] " All the decisions of the Council, provided that they be not an infringement or an alteration of the existing laws, are norms to be followed in the corporative organisation, and they are to be immediately put into effect by the Ministries and departments concerned." Its members are the President of the Council of Ministers, two University Professors, and a number of *ex-officio* representatives of various ministerial departments. This Council was created a year later than the National Institute of Labour and Social Welfare : and it seems possible that a little widening of the scope of that Institute might have made it unnecessary, so avoiding the creation of an extra body that has no representatives of the Corporations upon it. But no doubt the Portuguese know best.

IV

Having described the Portuguese Corporate State as it exists on paper, some mention must be made of what has already been done towards translating it into reality. I say already because the *Estado Novo* is coming into being surely but gradually. Plans for educating illiterate millions overnight, for bringing about an unheard of prosperity in the course of a few days, have always characterised Liberal and "progressive" régimes in the Peninsula; we have the example of the vast promises, so soon confounded, made by the Spanish Republicans in 1931. Or again, there was very soon a bitter irony about the rhetorical proclamation issued to the Portuguese people by the new Republican Government on October 5, 1910. "Now at last ends the slavery of our country, and, luminous in its virginal essence, rises the beneficent aspiration of a régime of liberty." And so on. The Republic had to give the people rhetoric, for it had nothing else to give. But there has never been any rhetoric about Salazar: his promises have always been most guarded, and the realisation more than the anticipation. First and foremost he is a realist: he is one of the very few politicians who have never allowed themselves to be mesmerised by words. "All one hears to-day on the subject of liberty," he has written, "or of Parliament, or democracy, or about the rights of the people and the brotherhood of man—all that has been standardised to such an extent that we shall soon be able to buy speeches ready-made to suit all occasions, as we can already buy love-letters."

"Wisely inoculated against the disease of extreme ideologies," writes M. Maeterlinck of him, "he admits nothing that will not stand the test of daily experience. His mind is a veritable laboratory, where distilled Utopias are made practical."[27] To quote his own words again, "The Portuguese Republic is a Corporate State by definition, but that does not mean to say that the corporative organisation is already realised wherever we have decided that it is possible and desirable. Far from it : we can have no rapid advance, but a slow and sure progress, as we are trying out a new system which has not yet been used sufficiently to make it possible to proceed without extreme caution."[28] Or again, in 1934 : " We are aware that there are grave errors in our economic and social organisation—unjust inequalities, imperfections, misery, falsities, and contradictions—and we have got to remedy them, or wipe them out. It is for that that we continue our revolution; but our revolution, if it is to be lasting, cannot destroy that upon which it is based—the fundamental principles, founded in the labour and the sufferings of past generations, the great realities of social life."[29] And in his famous speech of July 30, 1930 : " Because we are embodying our ideas in a Constitution, we must not jump to the conclusion that the remedy for all political evils is found. . . . It is not a programme for angels."

The reconstruction of Portugal has been and is being a slow matter of trial and error and patient endeavour, guided throughout by those social principles which we have tried to set out in the foregoing pages. Nevertheless, very considerable progress has been made, under the guidance of Salazar and his Ministers, among whom should Dr. Pedro Teotonio Pereira be especially mentioned.

The organisation of industry and commerce was undertaken first, being the most intricate as well as the most urgent necessity. The organisation began at the bottom : national syndicates and *gremios* came first. We have seen how in the case of the latter the initiative came in the first instance from the Government, as it had to; and how the workers' organisation was

the work of the workers themselves. Under the
" Liberal " régime, all Trade Unions were regulated
by a restrictive law of May 9, 1891; but there were
nearly 1,000 of them in 1930, before Salazar began his
work. There were so many because most of them had
no more than a purely nominal existence. It was
doubtful whether collective bargaining was permitted
by the law of 1891, even in its widest interpretation;
at all events, the general interpretation of it, which
certainly expressed its spirit, did not allow it. A decree
of December 21, 1924, anticipated the formation of
federated unions and the establishment of principles
for collective bargaining " according to the terms of a
further law "; but this further law never appeared, and
the decree was no more than a mirage. "One thing,
at any rate, is evident: collective labour agreements
had no binding force; there was no authority to ensure
their application, and apart from one or two isolated
and irregular examples, Portugal never knew them."[30]
The *Estado Novo* has meant justice for the labouring
Portuguese such as he had not known for over a
century.

Salazar has always put the working-man first. His
syndicates are now fully organised and fully effective,
and meet and collaborate with the organisations of
his employers. The "Unions" and "Federations"
described above are also in existence in many cases;
but the complete structure of the Corporations is not
yet achieved. Portugal is, however, more than half-
way from liberal-capitalist chaos to corporate order.

All that has been done in the various industries has
been described in detail, in English, by M. Freppel
Cotta, in his book *Economic Planning in Corporative*

94

Portugal. But there are two in particular, which concern between them a very large proportion of the working population, in which particular progress has been made: the industries of fishing and agriculture. These well illustrate the work of the new régime.

For centuries the men of Portugal have been men of the sea: navigators and fishermen. The calling of the sea is rooted deeply in all the history and traditions of the country; and the men of the coastal villages who catch fish are living to-day the lives that their fathers and grandfathers have lived before them through the ages. The new Government has not attempted to impose the full rigour of corporative symmetry upon this ancient industry: here are well illustrated its twin virtues of adaptability and the avoidance of bureaucracy. Particular plans have been made to suit particular needs. A special law, dated March 11, 1937, concerns the fishermen.

Employers and purchasers, owners of boats and others upon whom the fishermen depend, are grouped, as normally, into *gremios*. But for the men themselves there are not syndicates on the national plan, but special institutions called *Casas dos Pescadores*, Houses of the Fishermen, to which their employers and the owners of their fleets are also obliged to belong, and over each of which—there is one at every fishing port—an official corresponding to the English Harbour Master presides. The *Casa dos Pescadores*, then, includes both masters and men, and is designed chiefly as an organ of social co-operation. Its functions are classified under three heads: the representation and defence of professional interests; the instruction of the young in the art of fishing; and care for the sick, assistance for those who have suffered loss in storms, and general welfare work. It is something remarkably close to the medieval guild. And it is of the first importance to note the following clause in the law: " The *Casas dos Pescadores* have the duty of guarding jealously all local traditions and customs, particularly those related in spirit specifically to men of the sea." " As far back as the first half of the fourteenth century," writes Freppel Cotta, " the fisherfolk had formed admirable confraternities in which religious and moral welfare was combined with economic and social relief, and the influence of which was still visible in the prevailing rules of fishing, and generally in the customs of all the fisherfolk. Those confraternities were the accredited representatives of all seafarers, and were designed to help their widows, the sick and the disabled, and even to make good the loss caused by shipwreck or damage. Their revenue was derived from levies on catches or wages, collected and distributed as fairly as possible in a true Christian spirit. The *Casas dos Pescadores* have retained as much as possible of those confraternities."[31] Nothing could better demonstrate the essential traditionalism of the *Estado Novo*, which is in reality not a " New State " at all, but the ancient Portugal of history and the centuries.

The whole spirit of the new corporatism, indeed, may be found in this particular application of it. We see its traditionalism, its sympathetic power of adaptation, its avoidance of bureaucracy, and at the same time the recognition that the incorrigibly illiterate and unpractical nature of the Portuguese people, as well as the need for co-ordination, makes necessary the creation of a modicum of officials. The various *Casas dos Pescadores*, scattered round the coast, receive control from a central board, which administers their common funds, so that those in the less prosperous localities may be adequately equipped.

Fishing and agriculture, the two oldest occupations of mankind, together provide the livelihood of a substantial majority of the Portuguese. We have seen that it is the intention of Salazar to give to Portugal an agricultural peasantry of independent small proprietors. With this purpose, extensive irrigation schemes have been undertaken in the Alemtejo, in the basins of the Tagus and Sado rivers, where the rainfall is small and irregular, to make possible small-scale farming where it was not possible before. "We have already outlaid a million to initiate this irrigation policy," Salazar told Antonio Ferro, "and you will see that peacefully and quietly, without any kind of violence, we are carrying out a very far-reaching social work. What I say has been absolutely proved. In the north of Italy, for instance, and in the basin of the Ebro and other districts of Spain, the division of property by water has been successfully carried out; and in the east and south-east of Europe, where, especially since the War, a policy of distribution of the land has been followed by cutting up large estates as one would a piece of cloth, without regard for natural conditions, it is not difficult to see that that policy has failed."[32]

There is in Portugal, then, a large population of small farmers and agricultural peasants—a population which is being extensively increased. These men, the great backbone of Portugal and, indeed, of any country, are for the most part neither employers nor employed. If they are employers, they are employers only of one or two labourers; nor do they specialise but practise general subsistence farming. It is evident that they cannot be fitted into the general corporative scheme of syndicates and *gremios*; and this has been recognised from the beginning. In the very first article of the Decree-Law of September 23, 1933, which governs them, the *Casas do Povo*, or Houses of the People, are called bodies for social co-operation, and not simply associations for the pursuance of professional interests, like the syndicates. The syndicates also aim at social co-operation, which in their case, owing to their greater compactness and organisation, is more easily achieved; but they are primarily professional associations, vocational groups. The purpose of the *Casas do Povo* is to provide rural centres for social purposes. They are created on the initiative of the people themselves, or by the Government when it is thought necessary. All land-owners are obliged to contribute to their maintenance, and grants are also made by the State and by local administrative bodies. Their function is to provide social centres, assist the needy, educate the ignorant (a colossal task), and generally to raise the standard of rural life. They will make loans to peasants for agricultural purposes or for setting up small home industries, and provide unemployment relief, when necessary, in the form of work.

Provision has also been made for the creation of special agricultural *gremios*, to protect the interests of those who produce for market, and these can be organised into Unions and Federations. Commercial agriculture follows the general plan, and corporative organisation is well advanced in the production of the important products of wheat, wine, fruit, and rice. The same principles are being followed in every case: order is being brought into the national economy by that which is inappropriately enough called a " dictatorship "—it is a dictatorship which has declared for a policy of *laisser-faire*, but which will *laisser-faire* not isolated individuals but organised professions, autonomous corporations.

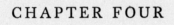

CHAPTER FOUR

THE POLITICAL STRUCTURE

I

IT is unlikely that those who are acquainted with the great social encyclicals of Leo XIII and the present Pope, and whose knowledge of the Portuguese *Estado Novo* is no more than they have obtained from the previous chapters of this book, will have any serious quarrel with the opinion of the American Jesuit who recently wrote that " the whole system is, in effect, an applied résumé of Catholic political philosophy and of the Papal encyclicals ".[1] The influence of these upon the mind of Salazar has already been noted; and Fr. Muller finds a " direct agreement " between *Quadragesimo Anno* and the Statute of National Labour.[2] The words of Pius XI in *Divini Redemptoris*, that " a sound prosperity is to be restored according to the true principles of a sane corporative system " might well appear to be an endorsement of the work of Salazar, and of his Constitution in which the influence of the encyclical of six years earlier is so apparent.

But there is more to the matter. Manoïlesco[3] rightly distinguishes three kinds of corporativism:

103

(1) Pure; (2) mixed; (3) subordinate. In the first the corporations constitute the sole source of the supreme legislative power; in the second that power is shared with other sources, such as a parliament based on universal suffrage; and in the third the corporations, with their organ of national integration, have only an advisory capacity. To him the only true corporative system is that of the first kind; and it is not possible to claim Papal approval for any system of political machinery. The Popes have not been concerned with politics, but only with the truths of religion and the moral principles which politics must respect, and which it is the business of the Church to maintain. The Church regards indifferently any form of government, so long as the essential moral rights of man are acknowledged and safeguarded. According to Leo XIII in *Immortale Dei*, "Not one of the several forms of government is in itself condemned, as none of them contains anything contrary to Catholic doctrine, and all of them are capable, if wisely and justly managed, of ensuring the welfare of the State."

Liberalism is a condemned error, because it teaches that "every man is a law unto himself", and because liberty of thought is in obvious conflict with Revealed religion. But the usual political concomitants of Liberalism—the doctrines of Parliamentary democracy, of universal franchise, of political toleration—do not stand condemned. And if Salazar has introduced in Portugal a corporativism other than the third of the three types distinguished by M. Manoïlesco, if there is in the corporative system any political significance, then it is something *more* than the corporative system of which *Divini Redemptoris* speaks.

And that is, in fact, the case. As has already been pointed out, the Portuguese corporative system is still in process of development, and it is not yet possible to say what form it will finally take. But it is already clear that the Corporative Chamber is to have more than a purely advisory capacity, whether or not it may ultimately be the sole legislative body. Moreover, there is every indication that it is to be the chief legislative body, and that the present undeniably authoritarian Government will give place to a form of organic democracy working on a functional basis through the corporations. It is at least certain that Portugal will not revert to Liberal parliamentary democracy on the English pattern; and before going on to discuss the present system of government and the possibilities of the future, we will explain why that is certain, by devoting a few pages to a brief historical survey of " democracy " in the Peninsula, and, in particular, in Portugal.

Rather more than a century ago, civil war came to both Spain and Portugal, where already the Napoleonic invasions had wasted and destroyed. In each case the war was one between rival claimants to the throne, one representing the traditional Monarchy, and the other (in each case a small girl) representing the ideas of the French Revolution, and heading what most historians term the Constitutional party. It was scarcely a generation since the fall of the Bastille. Particularly in the seaport towns of the Peninsula, those who saw political or financial power within their grasp played upon the war-weariness of the people to stimulate revolution. Don Carlos in Spain and Dom Miguel in Portugal were both followed by the greater part of their people; but the child Isabella in Spain and the child Maria da Gloria in Portugal both prevailed because both were given support from abroad by those who saw in " progressive " and " enlightened " governments possibilities of valuable trading concessions or lucrative fields for investment. A typical story was recounted recently with remarkable candour in a supplement to *The Times*,[4] in an account of the early days of the P. & O. Steamship Company, of which one Arthur Anderson was a founder. " The insurrection against the Queen of Portugal in the eighteen-thirties gave Anderson his first chance to show his mettle as a ship-owner. He and his partner came in on the Queen's side with all their resources, running cargoes of munitions and helping in every way they could. As a consequence when the rebellion was stamped out, they were given valuable trading concessions. Exactly the same thing happened shortly afterwards in connection with the Carlist outbreak in Spain, and the subsequent consolidation of their position in these two countries led Anderson and Willcox to charter several tiny steamers, the success of which enabled them to establish the first regular steamship line to Spain and Portugal in 1836."

There was no nonsense about non-intervention in those days. Canning, as British foreign secretary, knew just what Portuguese " Constitutionalism " amounted to, having earlier in his career been Ambassador at Lisbon for a short period, and sent out British redcoats to safeguard democracy. Palmerston allowed Pedro, father of the child-Queen, to enlist troops in the English workhouses, which were rather full at the time, and helped him to enlist them in Belgium. He also sent a British naval force in the cause, under the command of Captain Napier, R.N., an excellent British sailor and hero of the Syrian campaign of 1840, who on this occasion found it more convenient to be known as El Almiral Carlos Ponza.

Similar steps were taken to preserve Spain from Don Carlos. The British Government lent £540,000 to the child Isabella for military expenses, and gave permission for the raising of ten thousand men in England. The British Legion, under the command of Sir George de Lacy Evans, did not exactly cover itself with glory; but Palmerston's "inter-meddling", together with assistance from financial and commercial interests, was sufficient to ensure the success of political liberalism. The full iniquity of this work is to-day apparent; Spain is fighting again the same war, and the same international interests, together with others more deadly, are pitted against her. That Portugal is not also bathed in blood is due to António de Oliveira Salazar.

The war against Dom Miguel in Portugal, against whom, as Palmerston said in the House of Commons in June 1829, " the civilised world rings with execrations ", continued, owing to the strange preference of the Portuguese for tyranny, until May 1834, when he abandoned his claims by the Convention of Evora Monte. The child Maria da Gloria, at the time at school in Paris, was confirmed on the throne, and Portugal entered upon a century of confusion.

These are broad generalisations; and it is easy for over-simplification to become mere historical distortion. It is historical distortion to say that the Miguelist war was simply a conflict between national sentiment and foreign interests, in which the latter won. But it is also historical distortion to say that Spain or Portugal in any way desired or were suited to representative government. "One of the greatest mistakes of the nineteenth century," writes Salazar, with profound truth, "was to suppose that the English parliamentary system, English democracy, was a form of government capable of adaptation to the needs of all European peoples."[5] It is a pity that that historical fact is not clear to those well-intentioned Englishmen who so bitterly denounce General Franco as a "Fascist" and a destroyer of liberty.

In Portugal, as in Spain, Parliamentary government on the English pattern has always meant a chaos of *camarillas* and *caciquismo*, corruption, rotativism and revolution; it has meant the creation of a class of professional politicians preying on the people : a travesty of democracy screening the machinations of profiteers. That will seem like a sentence of excited exaggeration until the political history of Portugal in the nineteenth century comes to be written in English. English electioneering methods of the eighteenth do not bear comparison with those of Portugal. The electorate in 1871 was less than seven per cent of the population, and was wholly controlled, not by bribes, as in the good old English fashion, but by local "bosses".

The Portuguese of the years before 1926 cared little and knew less about what went on at San Bento, where the Cortès sat, and where (as he was always told) he was the ultimate controlling influence. "As disorder followed disorder, he turned himself always more deeply towards his wife and his children, his house, his daily work, the field, the garden, the forest. These things had been known to his parents, to his grand-parents, and to his ancestors through the ages, who had successively dug the soil, cultivated the vine and the patch of maize, reared children, suffered . . ."[6] What use was the "vote" to him? He was, and remains, an incorrigible illiterate, concerned only with the realities of life, with hardship and the soil, and with eternity.

"If Lisbon turns Turk to-morrow, all Portugal will wear the Fez," wrote the novelist Eca de Queiroz. Too often has the voice of the Lisbon mob been taken for the voice of Portugal. It was republican Lisbon that made Portugal a Republic in 1910; and the reasons why Lisbon was republican have been told in an earlier chapter. Only a few months previously King Manoel had made a journey through the country districts of Beira "which in some places became a triumphant progress, the peasants pressing eagerly to welcome their King".[7] But Lisbon turned Turk, and Portugal accepted, unprotesting, unknowing. For the last Ministry of the Monarchy, the elections of August 28, 1910, returned 14 Republicans among 144 deputies. Of these 14, 10 came from Lisbon. And when the Republic was proclaimed, the millions of Portuguese knew nothing of the matter, had no more hand in it than they had ever had in the affairs of Portugal, and were concerned in it only in so far as the fantastic confusion into which Portuguese politics were immediately plunged had its effect upon their daily lives.

The constant succession of revolutions between

1910 and 1926 were exclusively political in character, and were unnoticed outside Lisbon: the general disappearance of administrative order and the general rise in the cost of living continued steadily and without interruption. In 1926 the country rose: we have told the story already.

The Government that then, in the name of the nation, took control of affairs was a dictatorship. It was a dictatorship in the Roman sense of the word: that is, a Government that had seized temporary absolutism to meet a national emergency. It was certainly not a dictatorship in the modern sense of a tyranny: it represented a release from tyranny, from the intolerable tyranny of the professional politicians and the local bosses. At the beginning of 1928, General Oscar Carmona submitted his *de facto* Presidency to the country; on March 25th a popular mandate confirmed him in his office. Four years later a new Constitution which had been drawn up under the guidance of the Minister of Finance, Dr. Salazar, was also submitted to the country for approval. The plebiscite was taken on March 19, 1933, and resulted as follows:

Number of the electorate	1,330,268
Votes in favour	1,292,864
Votes opposing	6,090
Spoilt votes	660
Abstentions	30,654

The Government then ceased to be a dictatorship, since it became government through a popularly approved Constitution. It remained an authoritarian

Government, and one that can best be described as a Constitutional Monarchy.

I say a Monarchy because that word means the rule of one man. Salazar is a Monarch. In Portugal in 1926, as so often in ancient Rome, and as ten years later in Spain, it was the army that gave expression to the voice of the people. It was the army which gave power to Salazar; but Salazar was none the less far from being the nominee of a military Junta. He accepted office on his own terms, and since that time he has proved himself to be in the truest sense the servant of his people. Kings are sometimes the puppets of oligarchy, but Monarchs are always the servants of their people, and lose power when they cease to be so. A Monarch, by the support of the masses of his subjects, holds in check all those who in the nature of things hold high office in the State, and curbs the ambition of those who would turn administrative power to their own ends. A Monarch is the answer to the ancient question of Juvenal: *Quis custodiet ipsos custodes?* If he ceases to be the champion of his people, the balance is lost; authority passes from his hands, and the country is governed by oligarchy.

Portugal was governed during the nineteenth century, and during the first quarter of the twentieth, by a Liberal-Masonic oligarchy. But Salazar, who has eradicated both individualist Liberalism and anti-popular Freemasonry, is a Monarch: his rule is popular and national, and he would have been hounded from Lisbon years ago were it not so, either by the people, or by the dispossessed oligarchy appealing to the chimera of democracy.

To-day, then, Portugal is governed under a Monarchical Constitution. But there is every indication that this is only to last until the Corporate organisation of the country is fully developed, when the Corporative Chamber will become the chief, if not the only legislative body, and the form of government will become one that can be described as organic democracy.[8] The very fact that the present Constitution contains such ample provision for revision is perhaps an indication that it is not regarded as final.

We will, therefore, consider first the Constitutional Monarchy of to-day, and then the possibilities of the future. It will be interesting to see whether the Royal House of Braganza is restored. That may happen either before or after the present form of government is superseded. There is no heir in the direct line; but Dom Duarte Nuno, heir in the Miguelist line, is a young man, at present living in Austria. He is known to be in sympathy with the work of Salazar. It is not altogether improbable that in 1942, when the term of office of President Carmona comes to an end, the Constitution will be adapted so that Portugal can receive him back; then will the historic Portugal be fully vindicated. General Carmona is an elderly man, and is in his second term of office, having been re-elected (by an even larger vote than before) in 1935. It is unlikely that he will stand again. It is not impossible that in four years from now we shall have the Royal Houses restored both in Portugal and in Spain.

The restoration of the House of Braganza will not happen, of course, until all memories of the old party conflicts have been forgotten. The new Portugal does not tolerate political faction of any kind; it does not tolerate a Royalist faction. That is why, in November 1937, Paiva Couceiro, leader of Royalist disturbances in 1911, 1912, and 1919, was expelled from the country. But in a speech in 1932,[9] Salazar paid a handsome tribute to the memory of King Manoel and gave the impression that, when Portugal is ready, she will call back her Kings.

II

The Constitution of 1933 is divided into two parts. The first concerns "Fundamental Guarantees": it defines the functions of the State, the rights of citizens, the importance of the family, the principles governing the administration, and so on. In all that there is not likely to be significant change. Part II concerns "The Political Organisation of the State": it is that which we now have to describe, and which, as we surmise, may undergo revision in the future.

Article LXXI, which is the first of Part II, declares that "Sovereignty shall reside in the Nation. Its organs are the Head of the State, the National Assembly, the Government, and the Courts of Justice." It resides in the Nation, as distinct from being attributed to "the people"; that is, the old atomic liberalism has been replaced by a conception of society as an organic whole. It will be noted that although the Government is accounted an organ of sovereignty, the Corporative Chamber is not so at present.

The Head of the State is the President of the

Republic, who is elected by direct suffrage for a period of seven years, and is re-eligible indefinitely: a valuable means for securing continuity of policy is thus provided. By Article LXXVIII, "The President of the Republic shall be directly and exclusively responsible to the nation for actions performed in the exercise of his duties. In that and in his magistracy he shall be entirely independent of any vote of the National Assembly." He nominates the Prime Minister and other Ministers, who hold office subject to his will, and is empowered arbitrarily to dissolve the National Assembly "when the supreme interests of the Nation so require". He appears to hold very considerable power.

When we come to Article LXXXII, however, we find that "the acts of the President of the Republic must be counter-signed by the President of the Council of Ministers, and by any other appropriate Minister or Ministers, failing which they shall *ipso facto* be null and void". Three exceptions only are made to this rule: no countersignature is required for the appointment or dismissal of the President of the Council of Ministers, for messages sent to the National Assembly, or for his own resignation.

Article LXXXIII provides for a Council of State to act in conjunction with the President of the Republic on all important occasions, and to consist of the President of the Council of Ministers (to whom it is simpler and less confusing to refer as the Prime Minister), the Presidents of the National Assembly, the Corporative Chamber, and the Supreme Court of Justice, and "five public men of outstanding ability".

But it is not difficult to see that real power in the State lies with the Government, and that real power in the Government lies with the Prime Minister, despite the fact that he can be dismissed at will by the President. That is, real power in Portugal to-day lies with Dr. Salazar.

"The Government," says Article CVII, " shall consist of the Prime Minister, who may conduct the affairs of one or more Ministries, and the Ministers." Salazar to-day holds the Ministries of Finance, War, and Foreign Affairs, in addition to the Premiership.[10]

"The Prime Minister shall be responsible to the President of the Republic for the general policy of the Government, and shall co-ordinate and direct the activities of all the Ministers, who shall be responsible to him for their political acts" (Article CVIII). "The Government shall depend exclusively on the confidence of the President of the Republic, and their retention of power shall not depend on the fate suffered by their bills, or on any vote of the National Assembly" (Article CXII). Members of the Government need not be drawn from the National Assembly; indeed, "Members of the National Assembly or of the Corporative Chamber who accept ministerial office shall not forfeit their mandates, but may not sit in their respective Chambers" (Article CX).

The National Assembly is the nominal legislature, but all legislation of importance comes in fact from the Government, and there is every reason to suppose that the National Assembly is really intended—if it is to be retained at all—as a check on the executive. It sits for only three months of the year and any member has the power to initiate any legislation that does not involve an increase in national expenditure or a decrease in national revenue; any legislation approved by an absolute majority of the Assembly is submitted to the President of the Republic for promulgation, which may be refused. And all legislation of consequence comes from the Government during the nine months of the year when the Assembly is not sitting, in the form of Decree-Laws issued under Article CIX.

But if the National Assembly is not the normal legislative body, it has sufficient power to act as an effective check on the Government if necessary. For that reason it is probable that it will be retained. In the first place, if a law that has been refused promulgation by the President is brought up again in the National Assembly, and, being voted on again, receives a two-thirds majority of the votes of all members, then the President cannot a second time withhold his assent. And in the second place, a Decree-Law issued by the Government must come before the National Assembly when next that body is in session, and if ratification is refused, then it ceases from that day to be valid.

The National Assembly consists of ninety members elected by direct suffrage. An elaborate system of holding the elections has been devised to obviate the possibility of the formation of any political parties. There are no constituencies. At least thirty days before an election, complete lists of ninety candidates, signed by at least two hundred electors, must be submitted to the Government. The names on all such lists submitted, if considered eligible, are published in alphabetical order in the official journal, the *Diário do Govêrno*, and in at least two other national newspapers. On the day of the election, voters cross off from these lists such candidates as they may not approve, thereby voting for the rest; they may not add names that do not appear. The ninety candidates whose names are uncrossed-off on the largest number of lists represent the personnel of the new Assembly. It is never likely to be a very truculent body, since the Government can reject any candidate deemed ineligible, and among the requirements is a profession of fidelity to the régime.

The Corporative Chamber exists, according to the original version of the Constitution, " to report and to give its opinion in writing on all propositions or projects of law which shall be presented to the National Assembly, before the opening of discussion thereupon " (Article CIII). By an amendment of March 1935, the phrase " in writing " was deleted, and the Chamber was required also to report " on all international conventions or treaties ". In doing that it is clearly doing something more than providing technical advice on specialised subjects. Again, the Constitution originally laid down that it should sit only while the National Assembly was in session; but another amendment of the same date added that " in the intervals between legislative sessions, the Government shall be able to consult the specialised departments of the Corporative Chamber on decree-laws it is about to publish, or on laws it proposes to lay before the National Assembly ". Both these amplifications seem to show that Salazar intends that, when the Corporations are properly organised, and the Portuguese

Corporate State has got beyond its present transitional stage, the Corporative Chamber will be given wider scope. M. Freppel Cotta is of the opinion that " the National Assembly will be dispensed with, and the Chamber will act as the adviser of the Government, which will itself legislate ".[11]

That is not the opinion of the present writer: he prefers to think that the National Assembly will be retained, for reasons he has stated, but that the Corporative Chamber will become the chief legislative body. It is difficult to say definitely what is the intention of Salazar. In his speech of January 26, 1934, he spoke of the present position of the Corporative Chamber as " transitional"; and on December 9th of that year he delivered an important speech on the subject, in which he said definitely that he does not propose to abolish the Assembly " without the preparation of a long experience "; on the other hand he ventured the opinion that in twenty years' time there will be no purely political legislative assemblies left in Europe. We can but wait upon events. But it is at any rate clear that Portuguese corporatism, which gives the Corporative Chamber a voice in such matters as the conduct of foreign affairs, does not fall into the third of the three types distinguished by M. Manoï-lesco, and that it therefore represents something *more* than the " sane corporative system " recommended by the present Pope.

" With a lively apprehension of its responsibility before the nation—the embodiment of all the material and moral achievements of past generations—the State is profoundly national, popular without being demagogic, representative but anti-' democratic ', strong but neither tyrannous nor all-absorbing."[12] Those words of Salazar describe his intentions. He is against "democracy" in the sense in which Portugal has known it: he has eradicated political liberalism together with economic liberalism. But the essence of his Government is that it is popular, and it is inconceivable that M. Cotta is right in thinking that he proposes to give all legislative power to a government controlled only, and slightly at that, by a President elected every seven years. It is much more likely, whether or not the Assembly is retained, that the Corporative Chamber will be given something considerably more than a purely advisory capacity, even if it does not become the sole legislature, and that a real democracy will thereby be attained. The working of that democracy will be described in the next section of this chapter.

Those who disagree with or do not understand the idea of functional representation, and prefer a legislative assembly on the lines of the modern English House of Commons, would do well to remember that in its fourteenth-century origins the English Parliament was a typically corporative body. That is to say, its members were not elected by a few thousand miscellaneous citizens whom fate had placed all within the same geographical area, but represented the Estates of the Realm, and were called to advise the King on those matters of which, from their positions in life, they had particular and personal interest. The idea of corporative democracy is an older thing, even in England, than the Liberal democracy that was for a century so tragically copied in Portugal.

III

On June 30, 1930, Salazar delivered a speech to which the phrase "epoch-making" can accurately be applied, and which is "regarded as the Charter of the New State ".[13] The occasion was the founding of the *União Nacional*—the National Union—the organisation of those who, renouncing all party politics, have pledged themselves to support Salazar in his work of national reconstruction. In this speech Salazar, who has been Finance Minister for two years, but has not yet become Prime Minister, describes the principles which the future of Portugal will follow. It is the first important occasion on which he has publicly associated himself with wider matters than his immediate work as specialist in economics and finance : it marks his emergence as the national leader.

He is more concerned with the political future than with social principles. "We know only too well," he said, "that if the dictatorship were to go, and to give place to the rule of faction, it would mean the end of all the work of reconstruction, of all the possibilities of the present; the old causes of chaos and ruin would return, their destructive force accentuated by increased indiscipline, by exacerbated passions, by the collapse of all material and moral defences against disorder—even to the extent of undermining the conditions necessary to the very existence of society." It was true; a rigorous dictatorship was an absolute necessity, if life was to be carried on at all, in the Portugal of those years following 1926. Every kind of revolutionary and subversive activity was being carried on against the Government, particularly by Communists and exiled politicians of the old régime. The most formidable attack came in 1931, when riots and disturbances in Madeira, Portuguese Guinea, and the Azores involved a good deal of damage and loss of life. The plan was to make trouble in these places and in different parts of the country, so occupying the Government, compelling it to send troops abroad, diverting other troops to the country districts of Portugal, and laying Lisbon open to a *coup d'état*. Nothing came of it, owing to the fact that Portugal was solidly behind Salazar; and *The Times* was frank enough to say: "It is common knowledge that this trouble is the work of Portuguese politicians in exile in Paris, and particularly of some of the former heads of the Portuguese Grand Orient."[14]

The Dictatorship, then, was an absolute necessity; nevertheless, it was never regarded by Salazar as more than a temporary expedient, to give place to constitutional government so soon as the new Constitution could be drawn up, and so soon as the smouldering animosities of the old liberal party system should have sufficiently died down. "There is no doubt," said Salazar on the fourth anniversary of the national rising, "that the dictatorship, even considered only as a restriction to the Government of the power to make laws, is a political formula; but one cannot say that it represents the lasting solution of the political problem; it is essentially a formula of transition.

"Since dictatorships often arise from conflict between authority and the abusers of liberty, and since they generally have recourse to measures restricting freedom of association and the freedom of the Press, dictatorship is often confused with tyranny. That is not its essence; and if liberty is understood as the full guarantee of the rights of all—to my mind the only true conception of it—then may dictatorship, without sophistry, rival in this respect many régimes which go by the name of liberal. But it is in any case an almost unlimited power, and this fact makes it a very delicate instrument, which easily outlives its usefulness, and which can easily be abused. For this reason, it is important that it should not seek permanence."

That was in May 1930: and in the following month he made the celebrated speech to which we must now return, in which he outlined the theory of democracy which was to supersede the dictatorship when conditions should permit of it.

"The political liberalism of the nineteenth century," he said, "created the 'citizen'—the individual isolated from the family, the class, the profession, the cultural milieu, from the economic whole to which he belonged—and gave him the optional right of taking part in the constitution of the Government. It was there that the source of national sovereignty was assumed to be.

"If we regard realities, we find ourselves confronted here with an abstraction—an erroneous or inadequate concept—and it is in turning towards the natural groups necessary to individual life, and upon which political life really depends, that the point of departure which we seek will be more surely found. The first of these is the family, the irreducible social unit, the original core of the parish, of the township, and therefore of the nation. Effectively protected in its formation, its preservation and development, the family ought to exercise, through the voice of its head, the right of electing the members of the administrative bodies, at least those of the parish, for that right is no more than the natural expression of the hearths and homes, with the common interests which are theirs."

Article XII of the Constitution (quoted on p. 69, above) consequently describes the family as " a fundamental of political and administrative order, by its association in the parish and in the municipality, as well as by its representation in the local authorities governing these ". And Article XIX lays down that " the right of electing to the Parish Councils (*juntas de freguesia*) belongs exclusively to the families ". But by Article XXI, " In the political organisation of the State, the parish councils shall take part in the election of the municipal chambers and provincial councils, and in the constitution of the Corporative Chamber." Local administration is, in fact, the first interest of those specified in Article CII for representation in the Corporative Chamber, and at the present day it has more representatives there than any other. The family will thus be seen to be fundamentally represented in the Corporative Chamber: it has been called " the prototypal corporation ".

Continuing to speak of " the natural groups necessary to individual life, and upon which political life really depends ", Salazar turned to " the moral and economic corporations, such as the Universities, the scientific academies, the literary, artistic, and technical groups, the agricultural, industrial, commercial, colonial, and workers' associations"; vocational groups created, as he said, by the instinct of civilisation, and which, in the words of *Quadragesimo Anno*, "are considered by many to be, if not essential to civil society, at least natural to it". These, said Salazar, "should participate by vote or by representation in the Chambers, which we wish to be truly representative of the Nation. Once more we abandon a fiction—the Party—to make of a reality—the Association." And in Article XX of the Constitution we read: "All the component parts of the Nation shall be represented in the corporative organisations, through their appropriate organs, and it shall be their business to participate in the election of the municipal chambers and provincial councils, as well as in the constitution of the Corporative Chamber."

"To sum up," said Salazar, "we seek to construct a social and corporative State corresponding exactly with the natural structure of society. The families, the parishes, the townships, the corporations, where all the citizens are to be found with their fundamental juridical liberties, are the organisms which make up the nation, and as such they ought to take a direct part in the constitution of the supreme bodies of the State. Here is an expression of the representative system that is more faithful than any other." Or, as he wrote on another occasion, "In the domain of political institutions the corporative organisation is fundamental . . . the more this organisation is developed, the more will the State represent more faithfully than it does to-day the Nation itself, as an organic entity."[15]

So is the Corporative Chamber a body representative of the Nation. It is not merely a body representative of producers' interests : it integrally represents the Nation, producers and consumers alike. We have stated why we think that it is likely to become the chief legislative body in Portugal, and we have provided the necessary data. The reader must decide for himself whether he agrees.

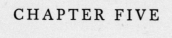

CHAPTER FIVE

CHAPTER FIVE

PORTUGAL IS NOT "FASCIST"

I

"DO not, I beg of you, compare the Italian case with the Portuguese," said Salazar to Antonio Ferro.

Portugal is not "Fascist". There is a very great deal of confusion about the meaning of that word. Owing to intensive and extremely effective propaganda from the Left, it has come to be generally and falsely used to describe any form of nationalism which will not tolerate international Communism, in the same way as it has come to be regarded by millions of muddle-headed Britons as vaguely synonymous with War. But there is only one country in the world to-day that is Fascist, and that is Italy. Germany is not Fascist; neither is National Spain. The reason, quite simply, is that Fascism is something Italian.

General Franco, when asked in a recent interview whether he was committed to the ideal of the Corporate State, is reported to have replied: "That is a general term, and may easily be misunderstood. Corporatism in Spain will grant to every citizen the right to participate in the social and economic life of the country on the basis of his labours. . . . Our corporatism, however, will be indigenous, domestic, Spanish. It will be suited to the individualism of the Spanish personality. It will not be slavishly modelled on foreign patterns. It should be noted, for example, that the system of corporations set up by Dr. Oliveira Salazar in Portugal is Iberian, not continental. We in Spain will fashion our own type of corporation." Earlier in the same interview he had said: "Obviously, the doctrines of the papal encyclicals furnish a sound programme of economic and social reconstruction. The application of their principles, however, must be considered in relation to the genius and traditions of the Spanish people."[1]

So with Salazar: the *Estado Novo* is not Fascist because it is Portuguese. But by saying that Portugal is not "Fascist" I mean three things more. I mean that the Nationalism of Portugal is not totalitarian Nationalism, in any meaning of that adjective, and that the corporative organisation of Portugal is different fundamentally, as well as in many unimportant ways, from that of Italy. I mean also that it is not true to regard Portugal in her external policy as an appendage of that artificial central-European *bloc* which is known as the Rome-Berlin axis.

The political problem of Dr. Salazar has been greatly complicated since civil war broke out in Spain. No government has better cause than the Portuguese to fear the danger of war spreading beyond Spain, and no government has more immediate cause to fear Communism in the Peninsula. This being so, it was impossible for Portugal to accept without reservation all the proposals of the International Committee for

Non-intervention. Because of this, and since there are certain obvious but superficial points of similarity between the political system of Portugal and that of Italy, whose interests in Spain are the same, she has been accused of deserting her centuries-old English alliance in favour of Rome and Berlin. She has been classed as " a Fascist country ".

Mr. A. L. Rowse, a distinguished exponent of Labour's views, put the common but quite unjust judgment on Portugal into one sentence in a letter to *The Times* in August last year (1937). He was maintaining that Europe is divided into two opposing and hostile camps, consisting of the Nations of the Right and the Nations of the Left. "In Portugal, even," he wrote, "it is a dictatorship of the Right which has deserted the old understanding with this country for a new one with Mussolini and Hitler."

But in point of fact, nothing of the kind has happened. Portugal is intensely jealous of her national integrity, and will repudiate any suggestion of external domination, from Italy or elsewhere, with the same proud scorn with which, in 1928, she refused to accept the Geneva loan. She is also intensely jealous of her now admirably administered colonial Empire; and Germany has not troubled to conceal her designs on the prosperous West African territory of Angola. If any further proof is needed that the judgment of Mr. Rowse was mistaken, it was provided at the Brussels Conference. Portugal has no important interests in the Far East, and she was able on that occasion to make clear that she is not subservient to the Rome-Berlin axis. Again, why has she not joined the Anti-Comintern Pact? It is because that Pact is a political mutual-assistance pact. Portugal is vitally concerned to fight International Communism, but she is not concerned in the political machinations of Italy, Germany, and Japan.

On July 4, 1937, a bomb was thrown at Dr. Salazar as he entered a Church to hear Mass, by men of the kind against which General Franco is fighting in Spain. Two days later he delivered an important speech to representatives of the nation's defence forces, who had assembled to congratulate him on his escape from death. In this speech he emphasised that the British alliance must necessarily always remain the basis of his country's foreign policy. "The most valuable item of our external policy is the age-old alliance with Great Britain; much of what we have done and intend to do still aims at tightening that bond. From time to time in Great Britain, certain persons, surely with no great sense of responsibility, irritated by our attitude in other matters (i.e., in Spanish policy), have placed their own passions or resentment above national and international interests, and have invited the British Government to reconsider the question of the alliance with Portugal. . . .

"We have special interests of our own in the Peninsula, and run risks which other countries do not share. We believe that public opinion in certain countries, especially in France and Great Britain, is ill-informed as to the true nature of the Spanish problem, and of the events that have taken place in that country. Some people do not believe in the Communist peril; we, on the other hand, feel it, see it, and fear that Communism, with the connivance of other countries, may take root in Spain, and so destroy any chance of the Spanish people working out their own political salvation—for there could be no national liberty or independent choice in a State largely controlled by several Internationals. Hence our uncompromising attitude from the very start: hence our opposition to any form of non-intervention which should prejudice the chances of Spanish Nationalism, which stands between Portugal and Iberian Communism; hence the odium which we have incurred in certain quarters—we may add, quite justifiably."

Portugal, then, unlike Righteous Russia, has never attempted to conceal the fact that she is interested in the Spanish issue. Salazar took the Ministry of Foreign Affairs temporarily into his own hands on November 6, 1936, when it became apparent that the war in Spain was to be a war of years rather than a war of months. His Government has done all within its power to collaborate in securing genuine non-intervention: it has scrupulously observed all undertakings it has made, and the amount of war material that has crossed the Portuguese frontier into Spain is less than negligible compared to the amount that poured across the Pyrenees all through 1937, unknown to those who know Europe only through the British Press. In October 1936, repeated accusations made to the London Non-Intervention Committee by the Soviet representative, M. Maisky, led the British Government to conduct an investigation of its own, as a result of which it reported to the Committee on October 24th that it had been quite unable to discover any evidence that Portugal had been the channel for the conveyance of any provisions, money, or arms to Spain. From the very beginning, the Soviet has made any real plan for non-intervention impossible. But Portugal, who of all nations can least afford to bind herself to neutrality, has honoured her word throughout.

The Communist Party in Great Britain is at present noisy but negligible; and it is difficult for the Englishman to realise the extent of subterranean Communist activity on the Continent, just as it is difficult for him to conceive that Freemasonry in Spain and Portugal is not the same respectable thing that it is in this country. He is inclined to utter a cynical "Pshaw" when he hears mention of the subversive activity of the Comintern; although he has by this time been sufficiently informed of the magnitude of the Communist *coup* in Spain which was forestalled by the Nationalist rising. The plan involved the creation of a Federation of Iberian Soviet Republics, to include not only Spain, Catalonia, the Basque Country, and the Balearic Islands, but Portugal as well.* The campaign against Portugal was made more urgent when war broke out; six million pesetas were paid by an agent of the Caballero Government to Portuguese agents, and the work of sabotage proceeded without delay. The Portuguese Legation in Madrid was sacked to facilitate quiet examination of its archives.[2] Next, in October 1936, revolutionary "cells" were planted on two Portuguese cruisers in a Spanish harbour, and a mutiny was engineered when they returned to Lisbon. The Portuguese Air Force restored order in half an hour. In January 1937, nine bombs burst simultaneously in the Ministerial buildings in Lisbon, planted there by six agents of the Okaba—a Balkan

* See p. 20, above.

branch of the Comintern, which specialises in such work. Little damage was done, and the *União Nacional* redoubled its vigilance. Finally came the attempt on the life of Salazar. It was not an isolated outrage, but an incident in a long campaign. The national solidarity of the Portuguese is proof against any serious Communist upheaval, but attacks continue. General Franco has successfully driven a Communist Government (in design, if not in name) from the Portuguese frontier. And it would be well for those in this country who denounce him so bitterly to remember that if he had not risen, and if International Communism had conquered Spain, it would undoubtedly have proceeded to the destruction of Portugal; and that, since Great Britain is bound by treaty to go to the assistance of Portugal should she be attacked, General Franco has probably saved Britain from armed intervention.

The Anglo-Portuguese alliance, alleged to have been abandoned, is in fact being at present strengthened by both parties by all means possible. The British are alarmed by the possibility of undue Italian influence in Nationalist Spain; if the Italians are to have the run of Spanish harbours, Great Britain is determined that the harbours of Portugal, which command the Atlantic approaches to the Mediterranean, shall continue to be at the disposal of the Royal Navy, as they have been for three centuries. Moreover, the alternative route to India and the East, by way of the Cape, is well protected by three groups of Portuguese islands: Madeira, the Azores, and the Cape Verde Isles. It is for these reasons that the Home Fleet is paying a visit to Lisbon, and that a British naval and military mission is visiting Portugal (February 1938).

Dr. Salazar's speech of July 6, 1937, reaffirming that the alliance of Portugal with this country is the basis of her foreign policy, was not reported in the British Press. But as Bilbao, Santander, and Gijon successively fell, and the Nationalist mastery in Spain became increasingly apparent, the general British attitude towards Portugal changed from one of rather suspicious indifference to one of emphasised friendliness, the principal consideration, as I have said, being the necessity of countering in advance a possible advantage to Italy in her bid for naval supremacy in the Mediterranean. About the middle of September, for instance, *The Times,* which is supposed to reflect official policy, started printing frequent testimony to the friendliness of the Portuguese, which, as its Lisbon correspondent was able to report, " created an excellent impression ". Dr. Salazar's speech was reported in its pages, more than two months late, on September 14th. It extended the cordial hand in a leading article on the same day, and in another leading article on December 10th. It devoted much space, and half a page of pictures, to the University of Coimbra, when that establishment began the celebrations of its four-hundredth anniversary. The first intimation of the mission that is to be sent to Portugal came on October 25th, and the official announcement was published on November 30th. On January 24th *The Times* produced another leading article, and another column and a half from its Lisbon correspondent. It is to be hoped that this visit will make it finally clear that Britain's oldest ally is Britain's ally still.

II

Portugal is not "Fascist".

Whether that word means the defensive tyranny of defeated capitalism, or the particular form of political and economic organisation to be found in modern Italy, still Portugal is not Fascist. It should have already been made amply clear that Portugal is not Fascist in the former, Marxist, and general understanding of that word. We will proceed to show that Portugal is not Fascist in the second and correct meaning of the term. Germany is not a Corporate State, still less Japan, although she is denounced as Fascist from Labour platforms. Italy alone is Fascist, and we are here concerned to contrast contemporary Portugal with contemporary Italy.

The obvious similarities are three in number. Italy is a Corporate State; so is Portugal. Italy is inspired by a strong nationalism; so is Portugal. And Italy is governed largely by one man, the head of the Government, who is known as a Dictator; so is Portugal. But each of these similarities is superficial; each of these matters is very differently considered in Portugal and in Italy.

The difference in corporative theory can be expressed quite simply: the corporatism of Italy is a *corporatisme d'état*, while that of Portugal, as we have explained, is a *corporatisme d'association*. Italian Fascism began with the compulsory dissolution of all existing forms of Trade Unionism; in Portugal there were no effective Trade Unions before the coming of Salazar, and, as we have described, the *Estado Novo* provided the worker for the first time with machinery for collective bargaining, which was not previously legal, and for the protection of his rights. We have noted the parallel between the Portuguese Statute of National Labour and the Italian Charter of Labour of 1927; but there are some very essential differences between the two documents. Article III of the Italian Charter of Labour runs: "There is complete freedom of professional or syndical organisation. But syndicates legally recognised *and subject to State control alone* have the right of legal representation of the whole category of employers and workers for which they are constituted." All of this can be found in the Portuguese Statute, *except* that key-phrase which I have italicised. Or again, in *The Corporate State*, by Benito Mussolini, we find the following: "The first legislative indication of the future development of Corporations may be found in the Act of April 3, 1926 (N. 563). . . . Art. 43 specified the character and nature of the Corporation, which was defined as an 'organ of the State' in the following terms: 'The Corporation is not endowed with civil personality, but is an organ of State Administration. The decree whereby it is constituted shall specify its organisation and regulate the duties of its central and local offices.'"[3] We could not better illustrate the precisely opposite natures of Italian and Portuguese corporatism. In Portugal, as we have already made clear, the Corporation is to be an autonomous body: we have quoted Salazar to this effect (p. 74 above). But in Italy, according to Mussolini, the Corporation is to be "an organ of the State". So can the matter be put into two lines.

To extend the contrast: Portuguese corporatism is integral, while Italian corporatism is exclusively economic. Integral corporatism, according to Manoï-lesco, is that which "considers as corporations endowed with an autonomous organisation and their own rights not only the economic corporations, but also the social and cultural corporations of the nation, such as the Church, the Army, the Judiciary, the corporations of national education, of public health, of the sciences and of the arts".[4] The Italian Corporations, to quote the Charter of Labour again, "constitute the unitary organisation *of all the forces of production*, and integrally represent their interests" (Art. VI; my italics). But the Portuguese Corporative Chamber is representative of the whole of the national life. It includes eight sections to which there is nothing in Italy to correspond: there are representatives not only of "the forces of production", but of the Catholic Church and her missions, of the national defence forces, of the Judiciary, of public and local Administration, of the Universities and Academies of Architecture, Music, and the Fine Arts, and even of the Portuguese Olympic Games Committee.

The contrast between Italian and Portuguese corporatism, then, is profound, and the similarities are superficial. Both are based on the principle that the common good is "more divine", as Aristotle and St. Thomas say, than the individual good, and is different in kind from the mere sum of individual goods; but in Portugal that principle is complemented by the principle that the State is the servant of society.

That essential second axiom largely explains the difference between Portuguese and Fascist Nationalisms. The nationalism of Portugal is a patriotism and pride born of her long centuries of history; whereas it is almost true to say that the exaggerated nationalisms of Italy and Germany can be explained by their lack of history, as nations. As we know them to-day, they became nations less than one century ago; and the *étatisme* of Fascist Italy and Nazi Germany to-day is largely, though not wholly, due to their anxiety that unity and national pride should appear to the world as their chief characteristics, since for centuries the peoples that comprise them had been so utterly disunited. But Portugal is a nation as old as Europe, and her present frontiers have been the same through eight centuries. Salazar is inspired with a sense of responsibility to history, to "our Lusitanian, Latin, and Christian patrimony"; and the *Estado Novo* is a vindication of the historic Portugal. That must be seized as a cardinal point if the work of Salazar is to be understood. His appeal is not an appeal to the vanished glories of the fifteenth century; it is not a political exploitation of the *saudade*. It is an appeal rather to tradition; it is a responsibility to the lives and sufferings of the past generations which have produced the present. As he sees it, the history of Portugal suffered an interruption during the nineteenth century, when the country was dominated by alien ideas and governed through alien institutions. Portugal for a period ceased to be truly Portuguese; but in 1926 that period ended, and the Portugal of history came once more into its own.

But if Salazar looks back across one hundred years, Mussolini looks back across two thousand, to the Emperor Augustus, whose bimillenary has just been celebrated in Rome with such ceremony. Mussolini also makes the appeal to history; but it is an appeal to the history of Imperial Rome, not to the history of the peasants and people of Italy; and it is the peasants and people of Italy of whom he is the ruler.

In support of that appeal, Italy must have also the impregnable navy, the vast army, the foreign adventure, the colonial empire, and so forth. The supreme necessity is that of proving to the world that she is a great nation. For that must her people be regimented, must freedom be destroyed, must blood be shed. That is the supreme mission of the State.

In Portugal it is not so. The mission of the State is to serve, not to regiment. Liberty is respected, therefore; and the Constitution lists and guarantees the rights and liberties of the citizens.[5] Subversive activity is not tolerated, but freedom of opinion is respected. "Personally," writes Léon de Poncins, "I was astonished at the extreme freedom with which opponents of the régime loudly proclaimed their criticisms in the public places. All of those who spoke thus of the severity of the dictatorship seemed well aware that if they said in Russia, in Germany, or in Italy a tenth part of what they openly expressed in Portugal, things would go very hard for them."[6] That was before the days of the Spanish war. "It was symptomatic of Dr. Salazar's régime," according to *The Times*,[7] "that, at least until the Spanish civil war, undergraduates might freely criticise the Government in the Coimbra cafés without fearing the presence of a police spy at the next table."

But the Spanish war has necessarily produced a state of semi-emergency in Portugal; liberties have

had to be restricted "for the duration". We have
spoken of the subterranean assaults that Portugal has
suffered at the hands of the Comintern; and the
Estado Novo cannot fairly be judged until the danger
has passed. Defensive necessity, moreover, has compelled various manifestations of Portuguese national
solidarity that seem at first sight to confirm the impression that Salazar is playing frog to Mussolini's bull.
The eleventh anniversary of the Revolution, for instance, was celebrated on May 28, 1937, in a manner
reminiscent of similar occasions in Rome or Berlin.
Fifteen thousand men of the Portuguese Legion, followed by five thousand boys of the *Mocidade Portuguesa*—the Portuguese youth organisation, so omin-
ously like the Hitler Youth and the Italian *Ballilas*—
marched down Lisbon's *Avenida da Liberdade* and
across the *Terreiro do Paco*, the famous Black Horse
Square, while ten three-engined bombers and fifteen
other fighting planes flew past overhead. But this sort
of thing only began ten years after the launching of
the new régime, and began, to the regret of Salazar,
to meet the first serious challenge the régime had
received—a challenge from without. With hell loose
in Spain, and the Comintern active; with the excitable
Portuguese mind restless at the sight of war; with the
Spaniards fighting for Spain and their existence—
there was no alternative. War in Spain began in the
summer of 1936. The *Mocidade Portuguesa*, membership of which is compulsory for all boys between
seven and fourteen, was founded then. In his interviews with Antonio Ferro, which provide the classic
guide to the mind of Salazar, he had said: "It is clear
that we neither can nor should follow the Italian sys-

tem of absorbing the child into the State, or copy the excessively nationalist and militarist organisation of the *Ballila*."[8] Similarly, Salazar had long been opposed to the foundation of the Portuguese Legion, a voluntary military organisation for the defence of the régime, which had long been urged by the more unbalanced among his advisers. He only permitted it when it became essential for the security of the State, and as soon as it was apparent that the war in Spain was to be a war to the death. Even so, it is by no means true that Portugal is living in a condition of permanent martial law, as Italy and Germany are practically doing.

"You cannot imagine how difficult it is to wake up our sleepy and apathetic race," said Salazar to Antonio Ferro. The function of martial music and military display can vary; and it is used to awaken the torpid Portuguese to urgent realities, whereas Mussolini uses it to intoxicate the electric Italian. But there are no spotlights on Salazar; Mussolini delights in the theatrical, but Salazar abhors it. His distaste for publicity is the despair of his officials. He attends two official banquets a year; for the rest, he emerges into the limelight as little as possible, speaks as seldom as possible, and leaves to President Carmona the business of taking salutes, inspecting guards of honour, and so forth. The only uniform he ever wears is a dark suit and a bowler hat.

The fact that Portugal during the last ten years has been rearming has again led to the facile comparison of Salazar with Aesop's frog. Of course Portugal is rearming. Even countries so pacific as Sweden and Switzerland are being compelled to strengthen their defence forces, with all Europe apparently treading the primrose path to the everlasting bonfire. And Portugal, apart from the menace from Red Spain, has great colonial possessions to defend, and listens with apprehension to the continual demands for Empire which come from Italy and Germany, those countries with whom her intimate co-operation is none the less alleged.

For three years past, Portugal has been drawing upon her fortunately stable finances for rearmament, purchasing aircraft and modern naval units in England, and other equipment elsewhere. Here, as in all else, she has to contend with pressure from International Communism, which caused the failure of a Czecho-Slovak firm to adhere to its contract, and the subsequent rupture of diplomatic relations, in August 1937.

In 1935 alone, £1,040,000 was spent by Portugal in British naval shipyards. Modernisation was clearly long overdue: until 1936, for instance, the flagship of the Portuguese Navy was the ancient cruiser *Vasco da Gama*, which had been afloat for well over half a century. When Portugal entered the Great War, the German paper *Simplicissimus* published a brilliant drawing with the title "The Portuguese Navy puts to Sea". That drawing well summarised the care shown for national prestige by the Liberal-Masonic hegemony that ended in 1926.

The Portuguese army, also, has been greatly improved by Salazar in his capacity as Prime Minister since, in his capacity as Minister of Finance, he made such improvement financially possible. It is now a very different force to that recently described by the late Brigadier-General Crozier in his book *The Men I Shot*. Its peace strength at home is 26,070, and in the colonies 10,000: small enough figures, in all conscience, but at least efficient. On January 4, 1938, an important series of decrees was promulgated, for the reform and reorganisation of the army. They testify, comments *The Times*, " to a courageous attitude by the Government in the face of Service conservatism ". They also demonstrate that the Government is not kept in power by the army, as its enemies allege.

III

Perhaps really the most important reason why Portugal is not Fascist is this: that Salazar is not a party politician. He is not, and never has been, concerned with political manœuvres. In Russia there is the Communist PARTY. In Germany there is the Nazi PARTY. And in Italy there is the Fascist PARTY. But in Portugal there is no party. Salazar is not the leader of a party: he is leader of Portugal. The *União Nacional* is not a party. It is not concerned with politics; politics have been banished from Portugal. It is the expression of national support for the work of Salazar; and the work of Salazar is to realise the national good.

" I laugh hugely," he once said to an interviewer, " when I hear talk of the ' Right ' and the ' Left '. In fact, I think that those words mean nothing at all. For my part, if you tell me that the Right stands for social discipline, for authority, for unity of direction —then I am of the Right. But if you tell me that the Left means an attempt to improve the conditions of

145　　　　　　　K

the lives of the people, to admit them to the cares of government, to raise their standard of comfort and education—then gladly am I of the Left. But the truth is, in my opinion at least, that there are no rights and lefts to-day; there are only plans of government, more or less practicable, that are either tried out or not. If they are carried out for the greatest good of the country, then a national work is done, and all the rights and lefts that there may be are therefore put aside."[9]

"When I speak of a 'National Polity'," he told Antonio Ferro, "I understand that the Nation—our Nation—is a living reality that we wish to preserve; that the Nation is an organic entity, composed of individuals differing in their abilities and in their occupations, which, dissimilar in themselves, make up a social hierarchy; that there are interests of this entity quite distinct from individual interests, and even sometimes conflicting with the immediate interests of the majority and, much more, with those of a group or class; that, for the good of the national interest, the natural or social groupings of men must be recognised—the family, the society, the Trade Union, the association for spiritual purposes, the local authority —but that groupings of a political kind, organised for the acquisition of power and the domination of the State, need not necessarily be recognised. These things are so self-evident that no party dares to pretend that it does not propose to bring about such a national polity, and all accept the foregoing principles —except such as concern themselves. Nevertheless, experience shows that they do not succeed in bringing it about, since in all national crises or in times of

general fatigue provoked by the party spirit, one hears
the cry that the party colours should be lowered in
favour of a truly national Government."[10]

He proceeds to emphasise that no Government can
govern truly in the national interest unless it completely transcends the party spirit, and actively
opposes any tendency of the party spirit to return.

It must always be remembered that he is talking
about Portugal, and that the *Estado Novo* is Portuguese. "I have not a horror of parties in a general
way: I have a horror of the party spirit in Portugal.
England has lived for centuries under a party system,
and has managed quite well so far. . . . But in Portugal these groups have formed themselves round
individuals or vested interests or seekers after power,
simply in their own interests. That is the sort of
party spirit that must be ended if we are to achieve
any real work of reconstruction."[11]

"The more profound is our feeling of the organic
reality of the Nation, the more necessary it becomes
to thrust aside all factions, parties, and groups to
which individuals adhere according to chance circumstances. There will be no more such politics, and two
benefits will result: for the Nation, the fact that the
Government will work solely for it, and for the
Government, the splendid liberty of being able to
serve only the nation."[12]

Contrasting the Portuguese with the Italian and
other revolts against the party system, he writes: "The
military origin of the Portuguese dictatorship will
always give a special characteristic to our revolution.
With us, it was not a party, a revolutionary force,
which seized power; it was the army, the voice of the

nation, which intervened to create the conditions necessary to the existence of a Government that should be both national and opposed to the parties. The armed forces do not constitute a party, do not represent a party, cannot depend on any party."[13]

The Portuguese experience has not consisted in the application by some triumphant faction of a programme previously prepared. What has happened has been that a completely disinterested Government has been placed in power by the army, and preserved in power by the gratitude of the people. The break with nineteenth century liberalism has been complete: that which has arisen is called the *Estado Novo*, the New State; but it is really very old, as old as Christendom and Kings.

Portugal, then, is not Fascist, for this reason: that in Italy, which is Fascist, a party with a programme gained power and applied it. In Portugal, a man with a number of fundamental principles, and those principles little more than the bases of Christian morals, was placed in control and fostered and developed a truly Portuguese Portugal.

There is no *étatisme* in Portugal: that is why Portugal is not Fascist. In rejecting Liberalism, Salazar has preserved liberty. He has preserved Portugal from any form of totalitarianism. To quote him again: "The State which would subordinate all without exception—its morality, its law, its politics, its economy—to the idea of nation or of race as represented by itself would come forward as an omnipotent being, a beginning and end in itself, to which all existences, both individual and collective, must be subjected, and would give rise to a worse form of absolutism than that to which the Liberal régimes succeeded. Such a State would be essentially pagan, of its nature incompatible with the spirit of our Christian civilisation. . . .

"The (Portuguese) Constitution, approved by popular plebiscite, rejects as irreconcilable with its ends all that proceeds, directly or indirectly, from this totalitarian conception. It begins by establishing the moral law and justice as limits to its own sovereignty; it obliges the State to respect its natural obligations towards the individual, the family, the corporation, and local government; it assures liberty and inviolability of religious beliefs and practices; it acknowledges the right of parents to educate their own children; it guarantees the rights of property, capital, and labour, within the social harmony, it recognises the Church, with the organisations which are proper to her, and leaves her free to carry on her spiritual work.

"It will one day be recognised that Portugal is governed by a unique system, which accords with her own historic and geographical situation, quite different from all others; and we wish it to be clearly understood that we have not put aside the errors and wrongs of false Liberalism and false democracy merely in order to adopt others which may be yet worse; but, on the contrary, to reorganise and strengthen the country according to the principles of authority, order, and national tradition, in harmony with those eternal verities which are happily the heritage of humanity, the appanage of Christian civilisation."[14]

Salazar, then, is fully aware of his European responsibility, of Portugal's duty of preserving her share of our common heritage of Europe and the Faith. And just as the corporative ideal synthesises all the various elements in the State, and disciplines them into one common harmony, so does it regard western civilisation as a wider unity, comprising different peoples, different cultures, and different national traditions. International co-operation, and the subordination of immediate national interests to the larger interests of Europe, are principles implicit in true corporatism. They are accepted by Portugal; they are not accepted by Fascist Italy. National self-sufficiency is constantly emphasised by Mussolini as an essential part of his policy. But Salazar has written: "There is not a single country in the world to-day that can say that it is open to the free exchange of goods; nevertheless, ours is among those in which the restrictions are least. We regard as a great error that extreme economic nationalism which we see arising everywhere, taking no account of the natural conditions of existence of the peoples, and destroying, to the prejudice of humanity, the special characters of the various national economies. Far from solving the problems of the day, the creation of self-sufficient economic units will serve only to create other problems in the future."[15]

The National economy of Portugal, which disciplines towards the common end all private interests, must not be confused with the economic nationalism of Italy or of Germany. She regards herself and her foreign possessions as forming a single whole; the colonies are "provinces d'outremer", and her first responsibility is to them. But her responsibility to Europe is always acknowledged. It is acknowledged in Article XXX of the Constitution, which says that

" the State shall regulate its economic relations with other countries according to the principle of appropriate co-operation ", equally as by Article IV, according to which " it is incumbent upon it to co-operate with other States in the preparation and adoption of measures designed to promote peace among peoples and the progress of mankind ".

NOTES TO THE CHAPTERS

NOTES TO CHAPTER I (PAGES 13 TO 30)

1 *de la Tour du Pin*: "Aphorismes de politique sociale." 3rd edition: Paris, 1930, p. 16.

2 *Divini Redemptoris*, par. 32.

3 J. M. Keynes: *The End of Laissez-Faire*. London: 1927, p. 41.

4 cf. G. M. Godden: *Conflict in Spain*. "It cannot be too often repeated that General Franco is Republican, and that he has never been a Fascist. In the New Spain the state will be corporative, and will follow on the lines of the Nuova Estado (sic) of Portugal." (p. 100.)

5 H. A. L. Fisher: *A History of Europe* (One volume edition), p. 659.

6 *The Times*: March 22, 1933.

7 Mihaïl Manoïlesco: *Le Siècle du Corporatisme*. (Felix Alcan: Paris, 1936). Quoted by M. Freppel Cotta in *Economic Planning in Corporative Portugal*: (London: P. & S. King, 1937), p. 16, note.

8 In 1935 there were 292 births and 176 deaths in Portugal for every ten thousand inhabitants. Both these figures are high; compare them with England's 147 births and 117 deaths. Between 1913 and 1935 the birth-rate in Portugal declined by twelve per cent; in England during the same period, however, the decline was thirty-nine per cent.

(Figures quoted in *The Tablet*, October 2, 1937, from the *Dossiers de L'Action Populaire*.)

9 Douglas Goldring: *Portugal*. London, 1933.

10 A. F. G. Bell: *Portugal of the Portuguese*. London, 1915.

11 These Chronicles have been published in an excellent English translation, edited by Senhora de Castro e Almeida. (Allen & Unwin: 1936.)

12 The phrase is that of Mr. S. George West, lecturer in Portuguese at London University, from his excellent lecture on "The New Corporative State of Portugal", delivered at King's College, London, on February 15, 1937, and since reprinted.

Further details of the financial achievement of Dr. Salazar are given later in this book, but those interested are recommended to read *Professor Oliveira Salazar's Record*, by Tomaz Wylie Fernandes (Lisbon, 1936: in English), or *La Renaissance Financière et Economique du Portugal*, by Paul Lavagne, in the *Revue des Sciences Politiques*, July-September, 1935.

NOTES TO CHAPTER II (Pages 33 to 67)

[1] Mr. David Hannay in the *Cambridge Modern History*: Vol. XII, Chapter X.

[2] A. F. G. Bell: op. cit., pp. 185-7.

[3] Sir George Young: *Portugal: An Historical Study*. (Oxford, 1917), p. 274.

[4] *Paris*: Gabriel Beauchesne et Fils: 1936. This book goes into an immense amount of circumstantial detail, and among other things prints the text of Law No. 1,910 of May 21, 1935, by which all secret societies were made illegal in Portugal, and gives details of the events leading up to that law.

[5] Young: op. cit., p. 286

[6] Senhor F. E. da Silva, in an address to the Société d'Economie Politique de Belgique: Brussels, December 1934. cf. also Paul Lavagne in *La Revue des Sciences Politiques*, July-September, 1935, on " La Renaissance Financière et Economique du Portugal ". " La guerre, qui imposa l'entretien de corps expéditionnaires, à la fois en France et en Afrique, n'aurait même pas, à elle seule, compromis dangereusement les ressources du pays, si l'ordre y avait été mis. La participation portugaise avait été financée par l'Angleterre et cette dette, portée dans les comptes pour une annuité régulière, aurait pu éventuellement faire l'objet d'arrangements plus supportables. Les bons du Trésor (87 millions au 30 juin 1919, au lieu de 1,250 en 1928) pouvaient encore être consilidés.

" Mais les extravagances financières, inhérentes à la période d'hostilités, laisserent dans tous les pays une funeste semence d'imprévoyance et de désordre qui trouva un terrain d'élection au Portugal. Ce furent alors l'abandon de tout contrôle, l'accroissement du gaspillage, la prédilection pour les solutions paresseuses, le fonctionnarisme hypertrophié, l'inccoordination généralisée la disparition des responsabilités; tout cela, favorisé par l'agitation incessante des partis."

[7] Bell: op. cit., pp. 213-15.

[8] Léon de Poncins: *Le Portugal Renaît*, p. 47.

[9] Ibid, pp. 47-9; Webster: *Secret Societies and Subversive Movements*, p. 283.

[10] *The Times*: March 13, 1935.

[11] Gonzague de Reynold: *Portugal* (Paris, Spes, 1936), p. 270.

[12] Antonio Ferro: *Le Portugal et son Chef* (Paris, Bernard Grasset, 1934), p. 178.
This book, a French translation of a series of interviews given by Salazar which was published in the Portuguese newspaper *Diario de Noticias* in December 1932, gives an admirable picture of Salazar and his ideas. Antonio Ferro is now head of the Secretariado da Propaganda Nacional at Lisbon.

OF SALAZAR

13 Ibid, p. 104.

14 H.-Ch. Chéry in *Sept*; July 1937.

NOTES TO CHAPTER III (PAGES 61 to 99)

1 This originally appeared in the Constitution as Article XIV. The Constitution has been amended in its details on several occasions: references throughout this book are to it as it was after December 21, 1936. It should be noted that the translation is the author's own, and not official; nevertheless he thinks and hopes that it may be regarded as accurate.

2 *Quadragesimo Anno*: par. 80.

3 *Divini Redemptoris*: par. 32.

4 Ferro: op. cit., pp. 133-4.

5 Pereira dos Santos: *Un Etat Corporatif: La Constitution Sociale et Politique Portugaise*. Paris: Récueil Sirey, 1935, p. 56. This is a long and documented study of the Portuguese Constitution, written as a thesis for a Doctorate at Louvain, and must be valuable to any who would study the *Estado Novo* in detail. It is, however, rather too minute and exacting in examination, since the Portuguese *Estado Novo* is admittedly only in an experimental stage at present; such a work will be of greater value when some sort of finality has been achieved.

6 Article 41 of the Irish Constitution (1937) begins thus: " The State recognises the Family as the natural primary and fundamental unit group of Society, and as a moral institution possessing inalienable and imprescriptible rights, antecedent and superior to all positive law."

And Art. 42: " The State acknowledges that the primary and natural educator of the child is the Family."

7 Salazar: Speech on March 13, 1933.

8 Salazar: Speech at Braga: May 1936.

9 Art. VI, 1, quoted above; also Art. IV.

10 Fr. Albert Muller, S.J., paper read at the International Union of Social Studies: Malines, September 1937.

11 Salazar: Introduction to the French edition of his collected speeches: *Une Révolution dans la Paix*. Paris: Flammarion, 1936, p. xxv.

12 *Quadragesimo Anno*: par. 95. See the encyclical " Non abbiamo bisogno " of the following month—June 1931—for a further discussion of Fascist Italy.

13 Gonzague de Reynold: op. cit., p. 310.

14 Salazar: Introduction as cited: pp. xxiii.-iv.
15 Gonzague de Reynold: op. cit., p. 311.
16 Fr. Muller: *La Politique Corporative*: Brussels, 1935, pp. 80-1.
17 Speech of Salazar: March 16, 1933.
18 *Quadragesimo Anno*: pars. 83 and 85.
19 Statute of National Labour: Art. VIII.
20 Ibid: Art. IX. Constitution: Art. XXXIX.
21 Freppel Cotta: op. cit., p. 153.
22 cf. João Lumbrales in *Politique*: Paris, May 1934.
23 *La Politique Corporative*, p. 88.
24 Statute of National Labour: Arts. L, LI, LII.
25 Art. II of Decree-Law No. 23,053: September 23, 1933.
26 Decree-Law No. 24,362: August 15, 1934.
27 In a foreword to *Une Révolution dans la Paix*.
28 Salazar: Introduction to the same, p. xxiii.
29 Speech on January 28, 1934.
30 João Lumbrales: op. cit.
31 Freppel Cotta: op. cit., p. 160.
32 Ferro: op. cit., p. 136.

NOTES TO CHAPTER IV (PAGES 103 to 125)

1 Michael Kenny, S.J., in *The Sign* (U.S.A.). May 1937.
2 op. cit., p. 65.
3 Mihaïl Manoïlesco: *Le Siècle du Corporatisme*. Quoted by M. Freppel Cotta in *Economic Planning in Corporative Portugal*.
4 Article by G. W. F. McLachlan in a special supplement published by *The Times* on the occasion of the centenary of the P. & O. Steamship Co. September 7, 1937.
5 Introduction as cited, p. xxxi. The following quotation from a speech of General Franco also has interesting bearing on the present chapter: " We do not believe in suffrage. The Spanish national will was never freely expressed through the ballot box. Before, first the political bosses and afterwards the tyrannical syndicates forced the Spanish people to vote according to their whim, giving them orders. The popular will in the new State will express itself through technical organisations and corporations, which, having deep roots in the country, will represent the genuine desires and ideals of the people. . . . Our Government will be strong—a Government for the people. Those who think we are going to support the privileges of capitalism are entirely wrong. We shall support the middle and humble classes." (Reported in the *Observer*: October 4, 1936.)

6 Salazar: Speech at Braga, May 1936.

7 A. F. G. Bell, op. cit., p. 194.

8 The present writer expressed this opinion in an article in the *Dublin Review*, for October 1937, which he sent, inviting criticism, to Senhor J. L. da Silva Dias, of the Secretariado da Propaganda Nacional at Lisbon. Senhor Silva Dias replied at length, disagreeing with several things, but without commenting on this particular opinion.

9 Salazar: Speech on November 23, 1932.

10 He assumed the Ministry of War on May 11, 1936, and the Ministry of Foreign Affairs on November 6 of the same year, both *par interim*—that is, to meet the emergency occasioned by the Spanish War.

11 op. cit., p. 25.

12 Salazar: in a broadcast: December 9, 1934.

13 Ferro: op. cit., p. 317. He prints the speech in full, but erroneously dates it 1928. The mistake has been copied by Gonzague de Reynold.

14 *The Times*: August 28, 1931. Quoted by Léon de Poncins, and translated back from his French by me. I have not had the opportunity to look up the original: de Poncins quotes a long cutting, beginning " Il est de notoriété courante que cette agitation a été fomentée par les politiciens portugais exilés à Paris, et particulièrement par quelques précédents chefs du Grand Orient du Portugal." op. cit., p. 75.

15 Salazar: Introduction as cited, p. xli.

NOTES TO CHAPTER V (Pages 129 to 151)

1 Interview reported in *The Catholic Herald*: Dec. 3, 1937.

2 The details of these events I have only on the authority of *Je Suis Partout* and *Le Jour*; but the general facts are common knowledge.

3 *The Corporate State*, by Benito Mussolini: Florence, Vallecchi Editore. 1936. pp. 96-7.

4 Quoted by Freppel Cotta, p. 23.

5 Constitution: Article VIII. We will list its more important provisions:

" The following constitute the rights and individual guarantees of Portuguese citizens:

1. The right to life and personal inviolability.

2. The right to good name and reputation.
3. Liberty and inviolability of religious beliefs and practice.
4. The free expression of thought in any form.
5. Freedom of education.
6. Inviolability of domicile and secrecy of correspondence, subject to the terms of the law.
8. No one shall be deprived of personal liberty or arrested without a charge being brought.
11. No one shall suffer punishment by perpetual imprisonment, or the penalty of death, except, as regards the latter, during a state of belligerency with a foreign power, in which case the sentence must be carried out on the scene of the war.
12. There shall be no confiscation of goods . . . from a delinquent
14. Freedom of meeting and association.
15. The right of property. . . .
16. There shall be no payment of taxes which have not been decreed in accordance with the Constitution.
18. The right of making representations or petition, claim or complaint, to Government departments or to any authorities, in defence of personal rights or general interests.
19. The right of resistance to any order which may infringe individual guarantees, unless they have been legally suspended, and of repelling by force private aggression when recourse to public authority is impossible."

6 Léon de Poncins: op. cit., p. 183.

7 *The Times*: December 10, 1937. In the matter of freedom to criticise the régime, it is interesting to note the methods adopted by Salazar, through the Secretariado da Propaganda Nacional, to inculcate his ideas into the nation, " The Secretariado classifies all periodicals according to their attitude towards the régime. There are those which are favourable, those which are sympathetic, those which are neutral, and those which are hostile. The Secretariado sends articles to the editors of them all. They have no obligation to accept them; if they refuse them, no steps of any kind will be taken against them. And here are some statistics: The Secretariado began its work in December 1933. Up to December 1934, it had sent 1,310 articles to 67 periodicals; from December 1934, to December 1935 2,027 articles to 75 periodicals. The number of neutral, and even of opposition journals which inserted articles supplied by the Secretariado increased considerably, and from the time that this work was begun the whole tone of the Press began to be more moderate. In December 1933, out of 251 political periodicals, 40 were for the Government, 61 sympathetic, 69 neutral, and 81 in opposition. By December 1934, out of 247 periodicals, 62 were for the Government, 86 were sympathetic, 43 were neutral, and only

56 in opposition. So do methods of persuasion generally succeed better than methods of constraint." (Gonzague de Reynold: op. cit., p. 307.) The only fact that dismays one is that there should be 251 political periodicals in a country of only seven million inhabitants!

8 Ferro, op. cit., p. 221.

9 Salazar, in an interview given to *L'Ami du Peuple*, Paris, March 26, 1936.

10 Ferro, op. cit., pp. 39-41.

11 Ibid, p. 231.

12 Salazar: Speech of October 21, 1929.

13 Ferro, op. cit., pp. 44-5.

14 Salazar: Speech of May 26, 1934.

15 Salazar: Introduction as cited: p. xxii.